Alphabet Soup

for Christian Living

Alphabet Soup for Christian Living

Susan McCarthy Peabody

Twenty-Third Publications
A Division of Bayard
One Montauk Avenue, Suite 200
P.O. Box 6015
New London, CT 06320
(860) 437-3012
(800) 321-0411
www.23rdpublications.com

The Scripture passages contained herein are from the *New Revised Standard Version of the Bible*, copyright ©1989, by the Division of Christian Education of the National Council of Churches of Christ in the U.S.A. All rights reserved.

ISBN 978-1-58595-599-2
Library of Congress Catalog Card Number: 2006936867
Printed in the U.S.A.

Contents

Introduction

Life is full of turning points with decisions to make at every turn, when our body, our mind, and our conscience may each tell us to go in a different direction. When my students seem to need it, I offer what I call "50-cent lectures." I'll give free advice if they listen! If a high school senior shows me her engagement ring, I urge the seventeen year old, "Maybe you should find yourself first. Go to college. Get a job. Then consider marriage. If the marriage is right, it will wait."

Years later, I see the students, some divorced with children, some in difficult marriages and others in sound marriages, some happily engaged in careers. I ask myself, "Did my 50-cent lectures help when they asked, 'How should I act? How do I decide?'" Questions like these are never easy to answer. We all need guidance. In our fast-paced, frenetic world, we seem to need a book of rules to guide us, like a book of "ABCs" we read when we were little. We need to know there are others who are in the same situation we are, or are at least familiar with it, and we want very much to believe that God understands, too.

For about thirty years I have kept personal files full of articles, papers, clippings, and artwork. These are subjects I have read and written about, seen, heard, and learned that mean a lot to me. As the years went by, I collected enough information to fill three file cabinet drawers. The files range from "Affirmation" and "Aging" to "Zephaniah" and "Zechariah."

After a time of serious crisis, when I felt that my dreams had been shattered, I was filing a stack of papers in my file cabinets. As I read some of the material, I realized that stored here was wisdom gained over thirty years of living and growth. The Scripture passages reminded me that God loves me very much and has a plan for me. The result of the collection is this book.

This little "Alphabet Soup" is a book of meditations applicable to our Christian life. Hopefully as you read these pages, you will turn to your own stored treasures. Choose a topic you're interested in or that you have a question about. Some of the reflections might make you laugh, and I hope so, since my standard advice is to lighten up. Or a certain topic might make you weep. If it does, then it has touched a tender spot, and that's okay. Our heart is a soft place where we have invited Christ to reside. He is gentle and has given us the gift of tears.

When my neighbor Mike, who has been with me through the process of "birthing" this book, suggested subject words for each letter, I sometimes rejected them. "Not fitting," I would reply. One day he made me pause when he asked, "What is this book about?" I can state what it's not. It's not doctrine. As I progressed through the alphabet, I realized this book is about some of the building blocks of Christianity. If you ask me, for example, to talk about Jesus, kids, prayer, Christmas or Easter, the Holy Spirit or sacraments, I might turn these pages and read to you what is in my heart. I talk a lot in these pages about what Scripture says on issues. Like those old 50-cent lectures, I open my heart to you.

"Well," Mike asked, "what do you want the reader to do?" What I hope you will do is review the contents, turn the pages, sample the topics; find something that grabs your interest. You've thought about a particular topic, and it is important to you. Perhaps the Thanksgiving and Christmas holidays are drawing near, and you want to read about them. Easter and Pentecost may be approaching, or you would like to observe the season of Lent with a special meditation. You might want to spend some time reflecting on prayer or kids, parenting or interacting with neighbors.

I hope you take something with you from this book. React, agree, or disagree, and don't be lukewarm about anything you consider here. Let your reading spark a response in you so you smile or nod in recognition. Write out your answers or plans to the questions and suggestions offered within the text and in "My Journal," a section found at the end of each chapter.

An additional tool is the section of Resources with more information about the books referred to or quoted in this volume.

I hope you also come to a deeper realization that God loves you beyond telling, unconditionally. Maybe you will come to see that you are the pearl of great price that God found and rejoices that you are his. God, who wants us to discover his love and be joyful, will not let us fail.

*God's love has been poured
into our hearts.*

ROMANS 5:5

Abba

New parents hover over their small child and listen to every burble from the fat little lips, waiting for the first word. "There!" shouts the proud father. "He just said 'Dada!'" "I don't think so," says the mother. "I think he has gas." For an English-speaking parent, "mama" or "dada" is the awaited word. For the Aramaic-speaking parents of first-century Nazareth, the word they awaited from a new baby was "Abba," meaning "father" in a very intimate sense.

The Old Testament closes in silence after the last words of the prophet Malachi, "Lo, I will send you the prophet Elijah before the great and terrible day of the Lord comes. He will turn the hearts of parents to their children, and the hearts of children to their parents, so that I will not come and strike the land with a curse" (Malachi 4:5–6). The people hovered in the silence for over 400 years waiting for the prophet Elijah. When Jesus started his ministry, he taught words of love and encouraged people to call God "Abba," my father. The Pharisees were shocked that a Jew would dare to call God "my

5

father," and they set out to find a way to get rid of Jesus, the blasphemer. Paul wrote that Christ's love, poured into our hearts by the Holy Spirit, made love our law, and in love we are enabled to call our loving creator, Father (Romans 5:5).

If you are not familiar with the wonderful hymn of praise called "Abba, Father," ask your music minister for the music and words of this hymn. Let Abba be the first word you speak or sing every day of your life.

Affirmation

Imagine you wake up each morning with a full sheet of clean white paper. You are sent out into the world with that new piece of paper and a pencil. "Go and do deeds of value!" As the day progresses, good and bad things happen. Does it ever seem the bad things outweigh the good? We are treated badly and are embarrassed. We fail in some ways, and as we hang our head, pieces of our sheet of paper are torn off in ragged bits. By the end of the day, we stagger home with a tattered fragment of the sheet of paper. This is our self-image. We are often unable to withstand the assault by competitive and sometimes unfriendly human forces, aided by our own self-doubts. This tattered image can become a part of our persona if we allow the negativity that afflicts our environment to affect us. We need to believe that what we do is truly of value.

This is where affirmations come in. If we are constantly aware of God's life-giving love and life-affirming promises, we can ward off the poisonous negativity that situations and people toss at us. When life seems cruel, and we feel we can't do good things and we're not valued, pray these words: "I am God's jewel of great value." Remember what Jesus said, "Come to me, you who are burdened…." Go on with your life knowing that you are appreciated, you possess dignity, and you deserve respect because you are a child of God.

Angels

According to the Bible and tradition God created angels a "level" above people because angels are pure spirits. Scripture records many cases where angels appear to give God's messages to his people, to strengthen their resolve to follow God's will. An angel visited Jacob to bring him a message from God, but Jacob struggled all night with the angel. God changed Jacob's name to Israel to indicate that a good man can struggle with God and live (Genesis 28:12–17; 32:24–30). The messenger angel Gabriel brought God's promise to Mary that she and her barren cousin Elizabeth would be with child. Gabriel advised Mary, "Nothing is impossible with God" (Luke 1:34–37). Scripture describes warrior angels whose mission is to protect the people of God, but the Letter of Jude reminds us that even the warrior Archangel Michael cannot kill but has to ask God to "rebuke Satan." The lesson we learn is that we cannot overcome evil by ourselves.

We believe in angels who defend us and bring us messages from God. Jesus told his disciples: "Take care that you do not despise one of these little ones; for I tell you, in heaven their angels continually see the face of my Father in heaven" (Matthew 18:10). Why not believe that an angel who sees God's face is bent over us, praying for and protecting us?

Anger

Unless you are an angel, you have tried different means to help you control the beast inside that sometimes foments like bile in an upset stomach. Even when anger is justified, it bears careful watching. A friend reminded me, "Anger is like drinking poison and waiting for the other person to die!" If we hold on to anger, it burns and hurts us. Peter tried to justify holding on to anger. "Lord, if another member of the church sins against me, how often should I forgive? As many as seven times?" Jesus answered, "Seventy-seven times" (Matthew 18:21–22).

Think of anger as a boat we tie up securely in the harbor of our heart, leaving no room for God to dock there. He wants us to let the anger go or to deal with it rationally, especially if it is justified and understandable. Have you ever tried to quiet an angry baby? You pick up the baby; you put your hand on his head and try to pull his little head down on your chest. Imagine God picking you up and trying to pull your head down to his chest. Try listening to God's heartbeat when you are in an angry mood. Trust that God will take care of things for you. Ask Jesus, "How do I get rid of this burning anger that overcomes me?" He replies, "When you put your head down on my chest, listen to me; love the one who offends you."

My Journal

- Learn the words of the hymn "Abba, Father" and reflect on them. Write down your reflections.

- How do you manage anger? Keep a record of your choices.

- Imagine you wake up each morning with a full sheet of clean white paper. You are sent out into the world with that new piece of paper and a pencil. "Go and do deeds of value!" Write about your experiences.

*Come, all you who are thirsty,
come to the waters.*

ISAIAH 55:1

Baptism

The church baptizes infants, children, and adults, making them brothers and sisters of Jesus and members of the body of Christ, the church. Through cleansing with water, then the anointing with the holy oil of chrism the child is purified of sin and sealed with the Holy Spirit. Jesus invites us to ask him for living water so he can pour it on us. He once sat at a well in Samaria and waited for an outcast woman to be open to his gift of living water. He promised her, "Those who drink the water that I will give them will never be thirsty. The water that I will give will become in them a spring of water gushing up to eternal life" (John 4:4–10).

Just as Jesus waited for the Samaritan woman, he also waited for Nicodemus, a Pharisee of the ruling council, to come to him at night so that Jesus could tell him the truth, away from the crowd of scoffing Pharisees. In the quiet and safety of the night Jesus offered the truth and the living water of baptism, "Very truly I tell you, no one can see the kingdom of God without being born from above."

9

Jesus told Nicodemus that asking for living water is a conscious decision adults make to turn away from the old life to a new life, being reborn, seeking the kingdom of God. To Nicodemus, Jesus affirmed, "For God so loved the world that he gave his only Son, so that everyone who believes in him may not perish but may have eternal life" (John 3:1–5, 16).

Jesus waits for us to come and ask for his living water. The prophet Isaiah spoke about the water God offers when he wrote, "Everyone who thirsts, come to the waters; and you that have no money, come, buy and eat! Come, buy wine and milk without money and without price....With joy you will draw water from the wells of salvation" (55:1; 12:3). To receive the blessing of this water, we have to want it, to ask for it. We have to leap into the water, drink and swallow it, and then it cleanses us. Doesn't it feel great to drink a cool glass of water when we are thirsty? Don't we love the smell of a newly washed baby? Imagine the smell of a newly washed soul surrendering to God!

Like the Samaritan woman and Nicodemus, we need to pray for Jesus' living water. In 1991, after a long time of being away from my faith, I was on a pilgrimage with my mother when a priest offered the opportunity for confession. Jesus was offering the living water without which we cannot live. Like the woman at the well with her secrets, I knew I couldn't hide. If I turned down the offer, I was turning toward eternal thirst and death.

I turned to God that day and I put out my hand and asked Jesus to walk with me. When God knocks, open the door, and open your heart to the Holy Spirit. Ask Jesus for a drink of living water. Take the water, drink it, and put your hand in his.

Beatitudes

The ways of God may often seem foolish. "Blessed are the poor in spirit, for theirs is the kingdom of heaven. Blessed are those who mourn, for they will be comforted. Blessed are the meek, for they will inherit the earth" (Matthew 5:3–12; Luke 6:20–22). I wonder how I can be meek, humble, merciful, and faithful in a world that rewards power and excuses violence and infidelity. If I keep trying to be a peacemaker, will the strong and violent just push me aside? How can I sorrow in a world that embraces laughter and parties and isolates or ignores sorrowing people? I'll be stuck in a cold, lonely apartment all my life unless I get out and dance at some parties.

In life, we can take one of two paths: the path of earthly reward, of satisfaction here and now, or the path of service, humility, non-violence, and mercy. If I pray and walk God's way, Psalm 1 tells me I will be firmly planted in good soil, watered, and well fed until I yield good fruit: "Happy are those who do not follow the advice of the wicked, or take the path that sinners tread, or sit in the seat of scoffers; but their delight is in the law of the Lord, and on his law they meditate day and night. They are like trees planted by streams of water, which yield their fruit in its season, and their leaves do not wither. In all that they do, they prosper" (verses 1–3).

To be "blessed" is to be full of joy and hope in relationship with God. Blessed are those who have directed their attention from earthly rewards, who have gone deeper than superficial thinking. They are examples for others to follow on the journey to find Jesus and the Father. If we feel we can't follow the path of the beatitudes, we can take strength from Gabriel's words to Mary, "Nothing is impossible with God." Pray for discernment and the strength to follow God's will and it will come. Write in your journal what benefits you have received by following the way of God. If you can't seem to think of anything you have received from God, then start to list the truly good things that have happened to you. Do you think you did all that by yourself?

My Journal

- Read and reflect on the passage of the Samaritan woman at the well. How does the living water Jesus offers affect your life?

- Write in your journal what benefits you have received by following the way of God. If you can't think of any you have received from God, then start to list the truly good things that have happened to you.

*Mary gave birth
to her firstborn son…
and laid him in a manger.*

LUKE 2:7

Christian Books

If you don't have the habit of reading Christian books, then think about Blaise Pascal's wager: "How can anyone lose who chooses to become a disciple of Jesus? If, when he dies, there turns out to be no God and his faith was in vain, he has lost nothing; in fact, he has been happier in life than his nonbelieving friends. If, however, there is a God and a heaven and hell, then he has gained heaven."

The same applies to Christian reading. If you don't spend any time reading Christian books or articles, or listening to audiobooks and lectures, you lose the chance to learn things that would fill the empty space inside you that you can't fill with DVDs and television. Seek topics like discernment, prayer, lives of the saints, or the pilgrimage of life, and you might hunger for more. Let the Spirit speak to you and stimulate you through the written or spoken word.

Find the Christian inspiration section in a bookstore or library. Look at the books and select one by the cover. I was captivated by the cover picture of a sculpture of two open hands on Henri

Nouwen's *With Open Hands.* The image of those hands can help us picture God as in the book of Isaiah, saying as we look into God's hands, "Don't you know I have carved your name in the palm of my hand?" Nouwen challenges us to a self-assessment. I wrote on the margin in the introduction, "What is my old sourness? What are my disappointments?"

The cover of Benedict J. Groeschel's *The Journey toward God* is illustrated with *The Journey to Emmaus* (Scala Art Resource), picturing the first Easter Sunday afternoon, when an erudite and humble man hid his identity from Cleopas and his friend but let them know him in the breaking of the bread, signifying the Eucharist (Luke 24:13–35). In a chapter called "The Dark Night," Groeschel writes, "Beyond the expected trials of any life of virtue there are specific experiences of darkness and aridity that are integral parts of the spiritual journey.... Their purpose is to draw us away from our own self-love and self-indulgence...and to help us become more pure in our love of God." When we are upset and angry in a dark, arid, and sterile time and we are suffering, we don't like it. God seems far away, but it is probably we who have moved away from God. We try to move closer to him as if we were walking toward Emmaus.

Holy Listening: The Art of Spiritual Direction by Margaret Guenther attracted me with a cover picture of two women lighted from below as if there is a fire between them. The fire warms them and provides the ever-changing light that fascinates and enables the reader to find peace by gazing into its depths. The book gently draws us into ourselves and teaches us to be still and to listen.

Guenther encourages us to discard what restricts us. "Play stretches us and helps push out the boundaries; in spiritual direction, it can provide gentle help in discarding icons that have become homemade idols....Play with the idea that God wants us to play." The author quotes Psalm 18:19: "He brought me out into a broad place; he delivered me, because he delighted in me." In the margin of that page I wrote, "Discard anger and intolerance." What idols do we need to discard?

A book for those who love history, the Bible, Jewish tradition, or just a good story is *The Gifts of the Jews: How a Tribe of Desert Nomads Changed the Way Everyone Thinks and Feels* by Thomas Cahill. Cahill asks thoughtful questions: What if the Jews had not kept the stories of the One who answered their every question with "I am"? What if the Jews had not obediently set aside the Sabbath dedicated to "a quiet weekly celebration of their freedom; leisure is the necessary ground of creativity, and a free people are free to imitate the creativity of God"? What if the Jews had not written YHWH (Yahweh), God's name?

Christmas

Scripture records times when God appeared to prophets or spoke to ordinary people. Moses recorded one of the visits when God came to live in the tent the Hebrew people prepared for him. Ezekiel wrote that he saw "the glory of the Lord…[that] filled the temple of the Lord," and he wrote that God left the temple due to Israel's sin (44:4). When we celebrate Christmas, we thank God for his real and tangible return, revealing his love for us in Jesus. During the Christmas season we sing carols about the little town of Bethlehem where a human child was born to a young virgin woman, when angels guided shepherds, and a star guided wise men to honor the King.

On Christmas Eve, make a mental pilgrimage to the manger in Bethlehem to worship the child Jesus and pray for peace for the little town of Bethlehem. Don't ask how the few of us can affect world peace with our prayer, but remember the angel Gabriel's words, "Nothing is impossible with God." With thoughts on Bethlehem and the Holy Land, use this prayer from Isaiah 2:4: "They shall beat their swords into plowshares, and their spears into pruning hooks; nation shall not lift up sword against nation, neither shall they learn war any more."

Confession

Who doesn't remember the story of the prodigal son? The young man in Jesus' story dared to say to his father, "I don't need you, old man; I can live on my own. Just give me my share of the inheritance now, and I'm out of here." The son took the money and left his father's home. Quickly he spent the inheritance on "wine, women, and song," and ended up starving in the most degrading circumstances. He realized he could do a lot better feeding the livestock on his father's estate, so he decided to bow before his father and beg for forgiveness. He met his father on the road home, but before he could get the words "I'm sorry" out of his mouth, his father swept him into his arms and took him back home.

Perhaps we, too, have been prodigal children, or we have children who left home in anger. We know that reconciliation can be very difficult. But our faith tells us that our Father in heaven has given us the freedom to conform to his will or not. If we should choose to go off on our own, we know God waits for us to come home. With this knowledge we can struggle to say the hard words of genuine repentance, but with the realization that God will listen and forgive us. "Father, forgive me for what I have done and for what I have failed to do." We pray these words at Mass or during the sacrament of reconciliation. Faith tells us to turn to our Father and express our deep contrition. He knows us and he waits for us. Before we speak the words, God will sweep us into his arms.

Try starting a conversation with God based on the Ten Commandments.

Have no other God. Do I love money and material things so much that I don't have time for God, that I make them my god? Does my pride keep me from lowering my head in adoration before God? Father, help me worship you rather than material things.

Do not take the Lord's name in vain. Do I honor the Lord's name? Do I offer my prayers in Jesus' name? Our Father…

Keep holy the Lord's Day. Do I reserve one day for worship, praise and study? Dear Jesus, I want to participate at Mass every Sunday.

Honor your father and your mother. Am I obedient to those who gave me life? God, help me ask forgiveness of my family for the times I have hurt them.

No killing. Do I respect my own life as well as the lives of others? Dear God, I ask forgiveness for whatever I have done to hurt others. May I ask their forgiveness.

No unfaithfulness. Do I respect my promises and obligations? Father, cleanse me and urge me toward fidelity.

No stealing. Do I cheat, take what is not mine? Father, stop me when I am tempted to be dishonest.

No lying. Do I gossip or "bend" the truth? Father, help me to speak the truth, and to use my speech to do good.

No desire for my neighbor's spouse or goods. Am I satisfied with what I have, or do I want what others have? God, may I be grateful for the gifts I have.

Love God. Do I offer God my whole heart, mind, and strength? Father, fill my heart with love for you.

Love your neighbor. Do I do what I can for my sisters and brothers? Father, fill my heart with love for my friends and for strangers.

Jesus invited little children to come to him because they have the humble attitude needed to approach God. When we approach our Father, we need to adopt a childlike attitude of trust in God.

My Journal

- Keep a piece of string handy. Cut the string into a three-foot length. Cut it in the middle, then tie a knot to put the string back together. Cut it again and make a knot to tie the pieces together. Repeat this step. Now measure the string. It is a lot shorter than three feet in length, isn't it? God holds each of us by a string. When we sin, we cut the string. But God ties it up again, making a knot. Each time we cut the string, God ties another knot, drawing us closer. Approach God and submit to his gentle will.

Hope in God.

PSALM 42:11

Death

"This is what death is," my friend tells me as she reluctantly takes pain pills that make her sleep when she does not want to sleep. Sleep is like death, or is it the other way around? Like a small child who tries to stay awake with the light on, we fight to avoid the sleep of death when what is calling us is brighter than any light we could ever know. I won't know what death really is until God calls me and reveals it.

Decision Making

The decisions we make are usually the result of choices we have made. Our lives are not stable, and there are many decisions we face—between this job and that one, between this person and that person, and between love and hate, good and evil, hope and despair. When someone lies to me, I have a decision to make. I can choose to take offense at the indiscretion, or I can forgive the person. I need to ask myself why that person feels the need to hide the truth from me. I can choose to focus on mending the trust between us. When someone steals from me, I can decide to forgive the violation of my property and peace, or I can hold on to my anger at the violation. When someone breaks my heart, I can choose to continue to love, knowing that love given is not always returned, or I can turn my back on love because I was rejected and hurt.

What do you think it was like in the Garden of Gethsemane that night long ago? Jesus could have decided to run away with the disciples, who would have gladly hidden him, or to face the authorities when they came to arrest him. Jesus chose to stand and have faith in his Father's promise of eternal life. He chose pain and death to show us his love and by his resurrection lead the way to eternal life.

Like Jesus, we have choices to make: to offer comfort or pain, nurture joy or sadness, provide love or hurt, give life or death. Choosing to give love and joy makes up for all the past hurts we have suffered.

At grave, life-affecting crossroads, don't make decisions in a vacuum. Consult a counselor such as the pastor, or a trustworthy group of friends, such as a prayer group or Bible study group. Make a list of pros and cons and listen to your friends as they brainstorm with you. You will always find an answer. You have the experts who can help you, and friends who can help because they love you. Read books by wise authors. Consult the teachings of the church. Above all, remember to pray and read Scripture. God is your biggest supporter and the best expert!

Depression

Most likely you have seen commercials for depression medications. One that I especially remember pictures people as little blobs. One little blob just can't seem to deal with the other little blobs. He mopes around. His life is not meaningful or happy. He needs an antidepressant. Other ads sell antidepressants but that poor little blob really stuck in my mind.

Most of us seem to fit in and act like everyone else because we are able to cope, but the signs of depression—sleeplessness, fear, anxiety, the desire to stay in bed, physical ailments, the petulance on the morning commute—can endanger relationships and our physical well-being. Depression envelops us like a blanket, heavy and wet with our tears. It can follow a loss such as the death of a loved one, the death of a relationship, divorce, a move, a loss of faith, retirement, or unemployment. Or a person may be diagnosed with chronic clinical depression.

When depression is caused by a loss, time is a healer. Whether you can link your depression to an event or a change in life or not, try reading psalms, praying, exercising, changing your diet and sleep patterns. If the depression continues for more than a week or so, consult a doctor who can help you discover what is causing so much emotional stress and can help you get out of the pit. Get away from stressful situations or commitments and set aside quiet time to listen to God's voice of peace and comfort. "Put your hope in God" because others can't make you feel better or make your life meaningful or happy (Psalm 42:2, 11).

My Journal

- Sleep is like death, or is it the other way around? Write your thoughts.

- Write about some of the decisions you have made recently. What steps did you take? Have your experiences taught you different ways to approach decision making?

Jesus said, "This is my body given for you."

LUKE 22:19

Easter

Easter is the celebration of the Lord's resurrection, when we rekindle our faith and light a new fire of joy. Remembering the resurrection energizes our Christian joy. Immediately after the Easter celebration, we are more committed to conversion of life and to living a more intense spiritual life. As the Easter season and the year continue, we need to keep up our Easter energy and commitment. Our lives are usually so busy and taken up with material concerns that we may forget our Easter assurances and the renewal of our baptismal promises. Jesus focused on maintaining his commitment to helping us and showing us what human life should be, and he changed the world.

Stop a moment and think about how you can remember your Easter joy and what you want to do about your experience. Create an "Easter Joy" section in your journal to help keep the spirit and commitment alive. Write some ideas for changing and following a more dedicated Christian way of life.

When I worked in youth ministry, I helped lead retreats called "Maintaining Easter Joy...Walk the Talk." Teenagers are full of energy, and they can teach us a lot about Easter joy. The theme of the retreats involved imagining situations we might encounter and talking about how to fulfill our commitment to Christian life by making the right choices. We talked about people who made the pilgrimage to the cross with Jesus, what we can do (become involved) and about our commitment to service (walking our talk). We recalled from the gospels that people had decisions to make as Jesus walked the Way to the Cross. Pilate chose not to become involved, and he washed his hands to be rid of an innocent man. Simon of Cyrene was pressed into duty, but tradition says he chose to commit himself and get his hands dirty for a man he didn't know. Carrying the cross with Jesus changed him forever. Like the centurion, Simon looked into Jesus' eyes and knew the condemned man was special.

We won't have the privilege of looking into Jesus' eyes until he welcomes us home at the end of our lives, but with faith we can see his eyes in the eyes of those who need us. In your journal write a promise to use prayer and reflection to strengthen your Easter commitment despite the anti-involvement message of peer pressure.

Eucharist

I find it amazing that I can attend Mass daily and love Jesus, but when asked to do some act of service, I turn to ice water and my feet are frozen to the floor in terror! For example, for at least two years my mother and pastor were asking me to become a eucharistic minister before I finally agreed to take part in the training. I learned that I would "serve the faith community in a way that is both a great privilege and a form of humble service...by distributing to others the consecrated bread and/or wine which has become the 'body and blood, soul, and divinity' of the risen Christ....You become one who serves, a servant, someone whose purpose is to nourish those who turn to the risen Lord for the nourishment only he can give" (Mitch Finley, *The Joy of Being a Eucharistic Minister*).

Soon after my training, at a weekday Mass, only two people stood up at the altar to serve as ministers of the Eucharist. The coordinator nodded at me, and I approached the altar for the first time to distribute Communion. As I stood in place to offer the Body and Blood of Christ, I thought of the words of my mother: "Say 'The Body of Christ' slowly. Look at the person receiving the Eucharist. Make sure the Host is firmly in his or her hand."

During the prayers at the consecration, the priest places his hands over the bread and wine. He is asking God, through the power of the Holy Spirit, to change the bread and wine into the Body and Blood of Jesus. Jesus promised he would be with us always, and we give homage whenever we approach to receive Communion or to kneel before the tabernacle, for he is truly present in the Eucharist (Matthew 28:20; Hebrews 9:11–14).

My mother tells a story that has strengthened my faith. Mother was very sick one autumn with chest pains and shortness of breath. She wrote to me, "I have a tale I must share with my daughters. Yesterday I felt so sluggish and had some problem breathing. But I decided to go [to church] anyway and say my prayers sitting down as I took my turn for Eucharistic Adoration. If I fell asleep I was sure the Lord would forgive me. At 5 PM, the person who was to replace me didn't come, and so I told May, who was also in church, to go home because she had to fix dinner for her husband who wasn't well.

"At 6 PM, the persons who were scheduled to be there at 5 PM came in, all apologies for being late. Amazingly, I was not upset and told them not to be. When I walked outside, I realized how much better I felt. I could breathe better. I turned to the chapel and said, 'Thank you, Lord, for giving me an extra hour with you.' Whatever happened during that hour I will never know, but I really have improved."

My Journal

- Create an "Easter Joy" section in your journal to help keep the Easter spirit and commitment alive. Write some ideas for changing and following a more dedicated Christian way of life.

- What has been your experience when asked to do an act of service? What would you do differently?

Be still and know
that I am God.

PSALM 46:10

Failure

We use the word "failure" when we don't accomplish what we wanted to do, when we follow a dream that eludes our grasp, or when we negotiate a place in a high-powered, fast-moving world and lose our footing. For a teacher, failure may be the inability to quiet a noisy classroom or to reach the students. For a concert pianist, failure may be the jarring note that disrupts the harmony of the orchestra. For a sales person, failure may be the empty showroom, the overstocked inventory, the unreturned phone calls. For a doctor, failure is the patient growing worse, the falling blood pressure after surgery, or the pale, drawn faces of the parents of a child who died during surgery. In our failure, we may beat ourselves up, soak in a feeling of worthlessness, or feel physically and mentally bruised. We burn with embarrassment and we "know" everybody knows the intimate details.

Failure fills us with the desire to disappear into the broom closet. If we're at the front desk or behind the teacher's podium, we look off to one side and whisper to ourselves, "They're not responding to me. What do I do now? I can't do this!" We hide and whisper a prayer in the closet or stairwell. "O God, help me here; I'm in trouble." But an answer does not come. In our panic, we are too noisy to hear God's whisper.

We find ourselves awake at 2 AM and writing plans for "how things should be done." We play concerts with our fingers in the air in the dark. We move our fingers toward the tumor in an imaginary patient. We close a sales call. At 2 AM we accomplish wonders. But by 8 AM, things fall apart. As we watch our early morning dreams wash away, we back off to our hiding place and ask ourselves, "What happened? Why didn't that work?"

We feel as though an "L" for "loser" marks our forehead, and we don't hear God's whisper: "I didn't hear you hit that off-key note," "I didn't hear loud noises coming from your classroom," or better still, "There was nothing you could have done to save that patient; it was her time to go." In our hiding place, the only thing we know is our failure. "I did not succeed," "I did not live up to my expectations," and worse than anything, "I didn't meet God's expectations."

People say they prayed, asking God for guidance. God answered them, and they moved in the direction he told them. Often, though, we don't hear our Father's directions, since our human hearing is not naturally pitched to hear the divine voice. We're plagued by questions, "What is God's will?" "Did I use my talents correctly?" Before a job interview we pray for discernment and ask for God's guidance. If we get the job of our dreams, we think that's God's will. If we don't, we're amazed at the failure, and we question God.

When I sit in judgment on myself after "failure," I reject the stories that Jesus told. Jesus talked about valued things, such as the pearl of great price for which a man sold everything in order to buy it. He used the parable of the coin the woman lost. She turned her house upside down searching for it. We've heard about the shepherd looking for the lost sheep. God assures us that he will protect and deliver us. He promises to love us faithfully but in our disappointment we forget that. Read the gospel stories of God's love in Matthew 13:45–46, Luke 15:4–7, 15:8–10. Scripture tells us that even if we do everything wrong and turn our back on God, he will not leave us alone. God is the Hound of Heaven, constantly pursuing us! If we squander the gifts he gives us, yet we turn back to him in repentance, he will run out to us, clothe us with a fine robe, and put a ring on our finger. When bad times hit, consider all we know about God's unconditional love, how God takes everything that happens and makes it right for those who love him. Where we land after our perceived failure might be where God intended us to be in the first place. God makes straight paths out of our crooked roads (Romans 8:28).

Faith

Some people believe that verse eight of Psalm 118—"It is better to take refuge in the Lord than to put confidence in mortals"—is at the center of God's revelation. God asks to be placed at the center of our lives, to trust that he will be there for us. "I can do all things through him who strengthens me," as Paul writes in Philippians (4:13). When in the midst of a catastrophe, resist telling God what to do and have faith! Say to yourself, "Forsaking all, I trust God."

Sometimes our minds are overwhelmed and all we can do is have faith and "hold on." In *The Gift of Peace*, Cardinal Bernardin relates his encounter with cancer. "I remember saying to friends who visited me, 'Pray while you're well, because if you wait until you're sick you might not be able to do it.' They looked at me astonished. I said, 'I'm in so much discomfort that I can't focus on prayer. My faith is still present. There is nothing wrong with my faith.'" Faith lives in the heart, even when the mind can't focus. While we read Scripture, we realize how awesome God is. Then because God offers us love, we yearn to return it. In our fear we desire to be close to God. We look over a great chasm at God, and slowly our faith grows. Faith bridges the gap to God, and in the stillness we hear his whisper, "Be still and know that I am God" (Psalm 46:10).

Father

When Jesus said "Abba, Father" and encouraged us to address God as Father, he wanted us to grasp that God is our loving Father. Embracing God as Father comes more easily to those who experienced a good relationship with a loving father. My friend Kathy says that her father's unconditional love helped her understand God's love. But lifting our arms up to God and asking to be raised up is often more difficult for those who have had a troubled relationship with their father. If we carry a burden of pain from childhood, our old, unresolved anger, fear, and frustration from our human relationship may cloud our relationship with God. We hide from what we perceive as God's wrath and retribution. We might even feel unloved, with the loneliness of an abandoned child. It might take many years to realize it was our father's frailties that hurt us, but with God's grace, childhood pain can heal.

In Scripture we find a God who lovingly waits for God's children to come home. The prophet Hosea, married to a prostitute, takes her back, cleanses her, dresses and loves her. Hosea's actions symbolize the actions of our loving God. Perhaps you see God the Father in Jesus' story of the prodigal son, in Luke 15. In this and other stories, Jesus beckons us to place ourselves into God's hands, trusting God to hold us gently and lovingly. Think of God breathing life into us to begin our relationship with him and to carve our names in the palm of God's hand. God created us to sing his praise with our lives, but when we are separated from him, we can't sing. God wants to be in our lives, to be intimate with us, to hear our voices in song.

Friends

I often begin a conversation with "My friend" as in "My friend said…" or "My friend advised…." I had a friend at work who usually started conversations with "My friend." She taught me how important it is to establish a heartfelt relationship with someone. The dictionary tells us a friend is someone who is cherished. The opposite of having a friend is being friendless or forlorn, left alone in distress, without hope, deserted. As a friend, we reach out and touch someone. We may not know who that person is, but it is possible that our new friend has been hiding behind a wall, what others call a mask. In befriending that person, we will be non-judgmental and respect confidences. We share with our friends the "Via Positiva," or the joyful way to the Lord. In putting out our hands, we offer to "lift up" our new friends, offering the tangible, healing presence of the living God.

A friend of mine has told me, "This is what a friend is: I don't have to wear a hat around my friend." If a friend's name comes to mind, write to that friend who might need someone with whom to step into the unknown. That friend always includes you in his or her thoughts by beginning with "My friend." Offer a word of sincere thanks for years of trust, assistance, love, and spiritual or physical support.

My Journal

- Write what this thought means to you: Faith bridges the gap to God, and in the stillness we hear his whisper, "Be still and know that I am God" (Psalm 46:10).

- Move close to God; let God speak to your heart and thank him for watching over you with love.

*The Lord is
at my right hand.*

ACTS 2:25

Garden

My friend Charlie showed me his garden. He picked and handed me a few cherry tomatoes to be eaten right away, there in the garden. I rubbed them a little and wondered, "Shouldn't they be washed? He's popping them right into his mouth!" Later after tilling and planting my own garden, I wrote in my garden journal, "I enjoy clearing the soil at sunrise when it is still cool. The work clears my mind for thinking."

"Heavy rains almost daily—need to wait until October to seed the garden!"

"Pulled up a carrot last night! Poor little misshapen thing! But I grew it! Very important!"

In gardens we can eat anything we want, and we can be alone to pray and reflect. Gardens teach us unconditional love and connection with nature. We learn that life is good despite the grubs, drought, heat, rain, fungus, and weeds. Green growing things promote the flow of oxygen we need to live, and they are a positive affirmation and reminder that life goes on no matter what happens. Gardens teach us patience and hope.

For hurricane preparation in South Florida, we bring into the house everything that could blow around during a storm. All my potted plants perch on top of filled shelves in the utility room. I don't bring them inside the house because they are potential homes for lizards, spiders, ants, and a garden snake or two. Too many of these creatures already come into the house clinging to the lawn furniture.

One year, when we had finished cleaning up after four hurricanes, I went out to the utility room to bring my plants out, but I found them brown and dry. I didn't fully realize how long we had been under hurricane warning until I saw those dead plants. However, I put those brown, dry, sad-looking plants on the front porch and gave them a good watering and lots of sunshine. Within a week they shed the brown leaves, and new leaves appeared. So life returned after the storm.

Goal Setting

If you ever make a wish, you might carry on this little lighthearted dialogue with yourself.

Self: "I wish I could have…I wish I could do…."

Other Self: "You didn't plan…."

Self: "What if I don't plan?"

Other Self: "You won't get there."

Self: "What do you mean by there? Where?"

Other Self: "I don't know."

Self: "If I don't know where, how will I know when I get there?"

Did you sing a song when you were little, a song you sing today with your children or grandchildren? "Twinkle, Twinkle, Little Star" or "When You Wish upon a Star." If wishing is all we do, we're in for a lot of heartache. Wishing is the first step, but making wishes come true takes a lot of hard work, including setting goals for ourselves.

I find it very helpful to follow certain steps in goal setting, and prayer is an essential requirement every step of the way. First, write a clear description of what you want and what you will have to do to achieve it. If you really want to change something in your life, you will want to have a clear plan to achieve your new goal. If you're not precise about what you want, you won't know what steps to take to realize it. You can set your goal by meditating on some topics in this book that you really like, writing about them in your journal, and beginning a self-assessment that will help you determine what your goal is. For example, write "What I like about the following areas of my life: career, personal, spiritual, and relationships."

First, work on small, short-term goals, then begin to think about the long term. Try to picture your life five and then ten years from now. As you consider what you have to do, ask the Holy Spirit to guide you in your goal setting and attainment. The Holy Spirit was present at creation, breathing life into the world, and was present at Pentecost with Peter, who waited in the upper room for inspiration, then preached boldly to the crowd, converting 3000 of them in Jerusalem (Acts 2:14–24). The Holy Spirit "spoke through the prophets" and continues to do so today, helping people do God's will. Go with the Holy Spirit and make wonderful plans!

Grief

Grief is an overpowering reaction to a significant loss, to a disruption of our lives when we are overcome by our emotions. In grief, we go into survival mode to protect whatever is left of our life. The event may be the loss of a loved one, a catastrophic community loss like that of September 11, a diagnosis of our own impending death, a divorce, or the loss of a job or a dream. We can't do anything but gasp with astonishment, like a fish that lands on a dock with no air to breathe. When the initial shock is over, we find ourselves walking around in a dark house, turning to say something or to share a thought but discovering no one there. Or we can't express what we are feeling. We seem to be looking down at nothing, and grief sweeps over us again like an airless tent or a blanket of soundless darkness. A pile of rocks seems to cover us, squeezing out all the air. But there is air, and we do survive.

Though we may not see it in times of loss, God created this world to be beautiful. God created our soul mates to be the object of our love, and created us to love mightily. God does not want lukewarm love from us. God wants us to passionately love both God and our sisters and brothers. If we have loved mightily, we fight losing the loved one, and we hurt to the core of our being when we suffer the loss of love. God gives us the gift of life. He wants us to hold on to life and fight for it. We fight death, and we rage against it, and do not give in until the end of our life.

Death's sting is powerful, vicious, and wrenching. As we trudge through the desert experience of grief, powerful emotions sweep over us: disbelief, anger, hopelessness, emptiness. We might shout at God, as the Israelites shouted at Moses as they trudged through the desert, "How could you do this to me?" They struggled and complained because they were hungry and afraid and yearned for the fleshpots they had in Egypt. Their lives were disrupted. They lost everything they had ever known, and they couldn't see any good in the Exodus experience. In this desert phase of grieving, we are isolated in our pain. We bargain with God, we deny the loss that started our grief. We believe if we stand still enough, we can go back home, or our loved one will come home, or our dis-ease will go away. We bargain, "If I do these things, then everything will be okay." But it won't be all right, will it? Eventually we must accept the reality of life. First we fight death and destruction, and then we realize we must put our life back together. Accepting the reality of death may be the first step in choosing life.

At this point, when we have chosen to make the journey of grieving, we need to think about forgiving our loved one for leaving us, forgiving life for turning against us, and forgiving ourselves for not averting the disaster, for the words we left unsaid and the hurtful words we spoke. Then we need to trust that what we are going through is normal, and that we will get back on an even keel again. We need to be patient with ourselves. This is the time when we begin healing. It is good to share with other people our fears and other feelings; we might find they have fought the same battle. As we converse with others, we discover they have experienced the same shaken faith, anger, fear, and loneliness.

In the solitude imposed by the grieving process, we need to find out who we are now that our lives have changed so dramatically. Finding a creative outlet will help us redevelop our inner resources and rediscover our essential self. We realize that during our desert experience, when we thought we had abandoned God in our anger, God was actually right there with us, sharing our pain. This discovery will probably stimulate a new outpouring of tears! But these are the healing tears that Jesus offers. This is the living water that we can drink once again. The process of healing is long and slow but ongoing. During it and because of it we can, with the wisdom we have gained in the life-changing process, help someone who has suffered a similar loss. We will discover we have come out on the other side of the desert alive, renewed, and full of faith.

My Journal

- Set your goal by meditating on some topics in this book that you really found helpful, writing about them in your journal and beginning a self-assessment to assist you in determining what your goal is.

- Write what you would like to change about yourself, what steps you have to take, and you are off and running.

When you send your Spirit,
you renew the
face of the ground.

PSALM 104:30

Healing

We can't retire from life and sit alone on the seashore surrounded by sand castles that protect us from hurt. We are bruised and even broken by relationships that send us limping blindly over rocky soil. We can bury pain deep in our unconscious, but untreated wounds poison the soul. We try to forget our pain until someone asks why we are so unhappy, tense, afraid, or out of touch.

Healing the bruised and broken soul sometimes begins at a retreat where we are immersed in discussions about Scripture that prompt us to ask questions about our relationship to the world and God. We discover we have entered a vicious circle. We have been hurt, so we closed ourselves off to protect ourselves, and our pain has become a part of our being. We don't realize we are afraid to open up again, so we can't be healed of the pain. We might have to give up a part of ourselves when we give up our pain. Guilt changes old memories, causing us to believe we did the wrong things and

36

that we can't be forgiven for sins long ago. We think we have caused pain, and fear takes hold of us, "What if I can't stop causing pain?"

When people approached Jesus for help, he would ask, "What do you want?" The paralyzed, deaf, blind, or leprous person would answer: to walk, to hear, to see, to be clean. Sometimes Jesus said, "Your sins are forgiven." These words spoken by a homeless preacher angered the Pharisees. When they and teachers of the Law asked him to explain himself with a miraculous sign, Jesus told them about a man with a demon. An evil spirit left a man and went into the desert, but the demon found the desert too uncomfortable. When the demon returned to the man, finding the man clean, the demon settled back in with some of his demon buddies. Jesus concluded, "The last state of this person is worse than the first" (Matthew 12:38, 43–45).

The story tells us that Jesus can heal our pain, but a person without faith can't keep the sin and pain from returning. When we are cured of our painful memories, burdens, and addictions, we have to replace "the old" by filling the space in our lives with new actions, plans, and thoughts so the old demons do not come back in increased measure. Jesus could easily have shown the Pharisees a healing miracle, but they didn't have faith in him. We can stop the vicious circle of pain and prevent a return to our former weak and vulnerable state by asking for the gift of faith. We accept that we are healed when Jesus touches us. In chapter four of the Letter to the Philippians, Paul suggests a way to accept healing: to pray and fill our minds with godly things and get to work (4:1–5). We are not just asking for a safeguard against our vulnerabilities, we are asking God to use us for his work. In keeping busy for God, we won't have time to backslide. If we pray, God will constantly send people to help and encourage us, until finally in an act of total submission we say to God, "I want to be healed forever."

Holocaust

"Lest we forget," a phrase engraved on many Holocaust memorials, helps us remember the millions of innocent victims and the hands that reached out to save a few of them. Lest we forget a father who was separated from his little girl at the train station in Warsaw. Her hand was immediately taken by someone who saved her life. Lest we forget a mother's hand placed across the eyes of her young son to keep him from seeing the ash and smoke coming out of a tower of death in Auschwitz. Lest we forget what horrors people did to others or what people chose not to see. Lest we forget what people do to other people in the name of unspeakable lies and what people do for others, by extending their hands and hearts to help them, often to the point of risking their lives.

Take the hand of an abused young child who can't keep his eyes from darting from face to face, wondering which child or adult will sneer at him and abuse him. Take the hand of an old person writhing in bed, frightened and alone. Give your hand to someone discriminated against. Take the hand of persons who are afraid of what they have done. Take the hand of one who is dying and who puts out her hand while she waits for an angel or the hand of Christ. How much does it cost you to extend your hand to save someone who wants to come in, away from the horror and darkness that only God, through your hands, can lighten?

Holy Spirit

Sometimes it's hard to understand our faith because we can't see or touch all the mysteries, for example, the Holy Spirit. We can't understand the Spirit with our minds, but we surely "know" the Spirit in our heart. That is our faith. If we were to ask artists how they wrote or painted such brilliant words or colors, they might say, with eyes wide open and looking as though they were struck by a great wind, "I don't know; it just happened!" Trying to define the

Holy Spirit is like trying to put our arms around the wind. In the book of Ecclesiastes, "David's son, king in Jerusalem," wrote, "I have acquired great wisdom, surpassing all who were over Jerusalem before me; and my mind has had great experience of wisdom and knowledge. And I applied my mind to know wisdom and to know madness and folly. I perceived that this also is but a chasing after wind" (1:16–17).

Stand outside and feel the wind. Is it a gentle breeze? Is it a hurricane? Breathe in the wind. Imagine your greatest dream. Is it to be a powerful artist, a great and beloved teacher, a famous inventor or skilled doctor? We believe that with the Holy Spirit, great artists, prophets, and apostles spoke and performed above ordinary human capabilities. Through faith, we know in our hearts that the Holy Spirit is this wind. Psalm 104 describes the Holy Spirit as the one who gives life and takes it away. "When you send forth your spirit, they are created; and you renew the face of the ground" (verse 30).

My Journal

- How much would it cost you to put out your hand to save someone who wants to come in, away from the horror and darkness that only your hands can lighten?

- Imagine your greatest dream and write about it. Then pray to the Holy Spirit to help you realize it.

*Jesus said, "I am the vine,
you are the branches."*

JOHN 15:5

Imagination

Walt Disney had great dreams. He created the Magic Kingdom in Disneyland so children and adults could experience the fantasy world of dreams and peace. Disney imagined creatures like the little dinosaur "Figment" and the dolls that sing in a small world. John Lennon wrote "Imagine there's no heaven," because he wanted to live in a beautiful, peaceful world. We know we have to wait for the eternal, peaceful world, the kingdom that Jesus promised, but it will come. It has, in fact, already begun here. And it won't be a fantasy, it will be real. Imagine the joy we will feel when we see God.

Throughout this book I ask you to "imagine." Imagine the smell of a newly cleansed baby. Imagine your greatest dream. Imagine heaven! Imagine the real presence of Jesus. Imagine yourself with Jesus. Imagine the joy of seeing the way to heaven! Imagine your heavenly Father smiling and giving you a hug for your acts of kindness. What must it be like to live in darkness? Imagine what would have happened if Jesus had said, "No, Mother, I won't do it until

40

they bring the water jars and ask me for help," or "I won't go to the desert until I pack some food." Suppose he said, "I won't go to Jerusalem until the authorities are willing to accept what I teach."

We can also stir our imagination by asking questions. How does life compare to a dance? What might Saint Paul say to you? Picture unity as all of us inside a circle of love and forbearance, and God's mighty hand extended over all of us, protecting us. Imagine the Holy Spirit hovering over your home as he did over the primal waters, in Genesis. How would you describe children drinking cool water that will quench the fires of anger? Imagine a short man's surprise as he climbed a tree to see Jesus, when Jesus looked up and called him with some urgency. This is not fantasy. The Christian can imagine all these things and more! Write in your journal what you imagine about Jesus and heaven.

Independence

Independence is a toddler taking a first step. We hold our breath and watch the child about to take a step or two. We want to reach out to steady her, but before we can, with a look of determination she takes her first step. Each step from this time forward will be a fight to learn to walk and to develop a unique identity. We will come into conflict with the child's desires over the years, but we have to give her the freedom to develop as an individual. If we try to direct the child every step of the way, we will damage the unfolding identity, just as we would damage a butterfly by helping it work its way out of a cocoon. Allowing freedom is probably the hardest thing a parent has to learn.

My friend tells me that she used to be "fiercely independent." I laugh at this because I have described myself the same way. What does it mean when adults say that? Youth and young adults have to struggle for independence, but over time circumstances can challenge it, and independence has to yield to pressing needs. My friend tells me people ask her what she needs. A year ago, healthy and fifty-two years old, she would have thanked the well-meaning meddlers and said, "Thanks, but I don't need anything. I can take care of myself." However, now my friend is sick, and she often thinks about what she needs. She teaches me about physical, emotional, and spiritual needs. She jokes when she says she has put her "Superwoman" suit back in the closet. Now she needs help with basic physical needs. She has complex emotional needs as she deals with pain. Her spiritual needs are becoming her focus as she discovers she needs the assurance of faith that a place is prepared for her in heaven, that she will be in God's eternal embrace. Together we talk about those persons whom she has cut off in the past because she thought their help stifled her. Now we decide that while independence is a good thing, interdependence is really more important.

Interdependence is part of life in a community; we depend on one another. We are all connected to Christ. We depend on Christ for our lives and we depend on one another to maintain life. Jesus told us in the Gospel of John, "I am the true vine....Abide in me as I abide in you. Just as the branch cannot bear fruit by itself unless it abides in the vine, neither can you unless you abide in me" (John 15:1–5). If we apply Jesus' statement to our lives, we discover that as branches united to Jesus, the vine, we can help each other get the sunlight and water we need to grow strong and bear fruit in our lives.

My Journal

- Imagine. How does life compare to a dance? Imagine a short man's surprise as he climbed a tree to see Jesus. Imagine these things and more! Write in your journal what you imagine about Jesus and about heaven.

Give to the Lord
glorious praise.

Psalm 66:2

Jesus

For twenty centuries since the resurrection, people have asked, "Who is Jesus Christ?" It is the same question Jesus asked of Peter, "Who do you say I am?" The responses are countless, perhaps as numerous as the persons themselves. The two men walking to Emmaus, in Luke 24, are lost in disbelief and disappointment that Jesus is dead. They listen to a stranger tell them wonderful things that Jesus said about the Messiah and the kingdom of God that is here already. They whisper, "He is a stranger...but listen to him! He makes our hearts burn!" (verse 32).

Jesus will walk with you, answer your questions, and comfort you. Early in the life of Theresa of Lisieux, she was graced with the knowledge that Jesus dwelt in her heart, and she let him take it over. She felt she could put her hand on her heart and touch Jesus. Jesus is the one who wants you to lean against his heart and realize he is in your heart. In a heartfelt prayer, Henri Nouwen wrote that Jesus is love that we can touch, "O dear Jesus, your heart is only love. I see

43

you; I hear you; I touch you. With all my being, I know that you love me" (*Heart Speaks to Heart*). Jesus is Love. Jesus is the Lamb of God come to retrieve a lost lamb. Our soul cries out, "Am I that lost lamb? Has Jesus sent me to comfort lost lambs?"

In *Secrets of the Vine*, Bruce Wilkinson paints a word portrait of Jesus as he takes us for an after supper walk with Jesus in the shadows of the walls of Jerusalem. (The parenthetical expressions are mine.) "They pass through ancient vineyards. They walk in single file between rows of neatly tended grapes, plants that have been bearing fruit for generations....Hemmed in by rows of vines, the disciples gather around (we pull in closer)....Jesus reaches for a grape branch. Showing signs of new spring growth, its woody stems lie across his hand in the golden light (look at the hand of Jesus cradling that branch). Now he begins. 'I am the true vine.'"

As branches on the vine, if I am covering you and taking your light, Jesus will gently move me aside so you can get light too. He takes a vine full of spring buds into his hands, just as his Father takes us in his hands. If we had been near Gethsemane that night, we might have seen Jesus take the vine in his hands and show it to the small group of men who were with him. If we cannot picture the face and heart of Jesus, we need only imagine the hands holding the vine, and know the real presence of Jesus.

Write in your journal about Jesus. You might create your own song or a word picture of Jesus. Try to see his face, feel his hands, hear his voice, hear his heart beat. Stay close to Jesus, breathe deeply, and say, "This is Jesus Christ!"

John

Everyone pictures Jesus in a different way. We want to learn more about the Jesus of the gospels to be assured that indeed he wants to be with us as we are, gritty, forgetful, and careless. And more than that, that he actually loves us! Saint John wrote his inspired gospel in such a way that we can actually see ourselves with Jesus. All we have to do is put ourselves into scenes with Jesus. Join me in this story that Saint John wrote in chapter four of his gospel. Place yourself in the position of one of the women or men in the gospel and see Jesus from that person's perspective.

The story begins at high noon in a small dusty town. You have just come to the town well from the desert. Your face and shoulders burn from the dry desert heat. Your tongue and lips are hot, dusty. Your eyes ache from the brightness of the sun and from the smothering sand that blows through your scarf into your face. You carry a water jar to lower it into the well for water.

A man sits on the edge of the well. From the colors and weave of his cloak you guess he is a Jew. As you glance sideways at him, your mind wanders, "What is he doing here at our well in Samaria?" He says, "Woman, will you give me a drink?" You shrink back. You are a Samaritan woman. The men of your own town will not speak to you in your current state, and certainly a Jewish man would never speak to you. Jews considered Samaritan women religiously impure. You hide behind your scarf and ask, "You are a Jew and I am a Samaritan woman. How can you ask me for a drink?"

Look at him. A gentle, respectful, Jewish man who sits by a well on a hot day and speaks to an outcast Samaritan woman. His hand caresses the stone of the old well. When he speaks, a cool breeze blows. As you converse with him, you struggle with the truth. Your mind returns to a memory of Jacob who struggled with God. You are dissembling about your life. You are impure, but you won't admit it, and this man knows it. The young man turns the tables of the conversation, offering "living water" to the woman with the water jar.

How will you write the end of this scene for yourself? The woman leaves her prized possession, the water jar, and runs to testify to the people in town that she has spoken with the Messiah. Her joy at meeting the Messiah inspires her to speak about him, and they believe her. Imagine the young man at the well. He offers the water to you, to your heart. He offers truth and life to an outcast.

By playing a part in this scene, like Jacob who struggled with an angel and like the Samaritan woman, you discover your relationship with God. You discover you can't sneak past God on your way to the well. You can't lie to God, and he has gifts for you no matter what you've done! Like Moses, you discover that you have "seen God face to face, and yet my life is preserved" (John 4:4–9; Genesis 32:30). You discover that being face to face with God is like being under the noonday sun.

Under the white hot gaze of the Son the Samaritan woman's heart melted. Just as we would do, she asked for a miracle, "Give me this living water so that I won't get thirsty and have to keep coming here to draw water." In return, Jesus told the woman, "You won't ever get thirsty again if you drink the life-giving water I offer you."

The Gospel of John is unparalleled, like a love poem that gives us a living picture of Jesus, life and light (John 1:4–5), who lived among us as a man and who promises life that cannot be extinguished. John helps us discover Jesus. In your journal describe the scene of your discovery of Jesus. As clearly as possible use the storytelling and poetry style that John uses.

Joy

Listen to a teenager say the word "awesome!" They use the word with abandon and joy. Awesome comes from a word that means fear and amazement. You can't say the word "awe" with your mouth closed. Try it. "Awe." Your mouth forms a circle and your eyes widen as your forehead lifts. You can feel the reverence in the word. To me, "joy" is like saying "awe." I like to look down a road that has trees on both sides. I face the wind and ride down that road with joy. Joy involves looking up at the stars on a clear night. It means watching a baby's birth and listening to the first lusty cry as the baby feels the cool air for the first time.

Listen to the psalmist as he sings, "Make a joyful noise to God, all the earth; sing the glory of his name; give to him glorious praise. Say to God, 'How awesome are your deeds!'" (Psalm 66:1–4).

Joy is what Jacob felt looking up to see a stairway with angels walking up and down (Genesis 28:12–13). Imagine the joy of seeing the way to heaven! Joy is what Elijah felt standing on the edge of the cliff when God whispered to him in a grand and portentous silence (1 Kings 19:11–14). Joy is being alone with God in the privacy of a mountain top. Joy is claiming Jesus' promise, "If you keep my commandments, you will abide in my love…so that my joy may be in you, and that your joy may be complete" (John 15:10–11). The great joy of our life will come when we see God, as Paul describes it: "Now we see in a mirror, dimly…[then] face to face," when God takes our hand in his and all that is separated is united again (1 Corinthians 13:12).

My Journal

- John helps us discover Jesus. Who do you think Jesus is? Read what others have said about Jesus. See him from the perspective of a gospel author or figure.

- What does joy mean to you? How can you share and spread it?

Those who fear the Lord
prepare their hearts.

Sirach 2:17

Kids

Neighbors and I have debated what to call young people. They're not children. We could call them "young adults," but they're not anywhere near adulthood, so the word "kids" sticks. "You have to write about youth. They are the most important topic you can have in *Alphabet Soup*," my neighbor insists, as she laughs and tickles her two-year-old's chin.

Despite the protective mechanism in mothers who often try to shield their children, many kids are lost and even "thrown away" as their parents become enmeshed in their own complex troubles. Teenagers are vulnerable to self-image problems. They fall prey to our national epidemic of drinking, drugs, and sexual abuse. Often they are innocent victims caught in the vortex of violent crime that many neighborhoods are subject to. Youth today have seen buildings blown up and cars crushed in roadside bombings, all in the name of religious war and insurrection. They know how to get on Web sites that are full of graphic hatred. They have assumed a tough mantle to protect themselves. In a many-cultured world, crowded into cities and classrooms with dwindling resources, violence erupts. We can't always shield our children, but we can encourage them to deal with conflict through nonviolent interaction and peaceful ways.

Despite the fact that our youth seem to speak a foreign language, it is urgent to communicate with them. Get down on the floor and play with them or sit with them. Listen to what interests them, but most of all, talk with them. A child might reveal fear of a bully or someone with a gun. The fear, pain, or anger of our youth can be deep and consuming. We can help them understand that adults share the same types of feelings. Youth are human persons, too, just smaller, less mature, and a little more frightened than we are. Our youth are the hope of the future. So let's listen to them. They might think that we are too harsh. They want us to stop domestic and verbal violence; they want us to read with them rather than sitting them in front of the television. Start by going to a library or bookstore and watch your youth take books off the shelves. Adults can greatly improve their kid's chances of living the life God intended for them. Which story will you read with them tonight?

Kindness

One fish jumps.
Endless circles begin.
One fish touches infinity.
When I watched a fish jump, I wondered where the ripples stopped. The circles the jumping fish makes in the water continue out from the center in a series of widening circles. Like those circles in the water, our actions never stop having an effect across time. Our actions cause other actions, and so on indefinitely. If we believe that the best thing we can ever do is to answer every action with an act of kindness, those kind acts would repeat through infinity.

The root word of "kindness" is related to "kin," of the same family or clan. In ancient days, rules were drawn up to be followed within the clan to protect the health and longevity of the group. Wouldn't kindness today protect the health of our parish community and of society? Wouldn't it be great if we could tell God our Father something positive when he asks us, "What kindness did you do for someone today?" Wouldn't it be wonderful to tell him the simple acts of kindness we did? "I loaded groceries into an elderly woman's car. I said 'Please' and 'Thank you' many times today. I brought the widow's newspaper to the front door so she wouldn't have to go out in the snow. I fixed the retired man's fence. I repaired a child's bicycle chain. I weeded the minister's garden. I visited a sick man who can't go to Sunday Mass and told him about the pastor's homily. I visited prisoners to talk about Scripture. I cooked for the homeless. I babysat for a child whose mother needed a break. I did not return an insult that was hurled at me in anger. I forgave a classmate who hit me."

Do you beam with joy when you recite this list? Imagine that God would beam and maybe hug us for our acts of kindness. Some of our actions will be visible, and some will be nameless and anonymous. Both will ripple out into the universe and keep touching people on into infinity. What kindness did you do for someone today?

Knowledge

Knowledge is grasping information, taking facts into the mind and then storing them. Human beings hunger for knowledge. We stand on the earth and ask, "How was the universe formed? How was life created? What is the purpose of life?" Our search for knowledge often leads us into a lifetime of study, and there can be disastrous results if the search is conducted without the awareness that all things are from God and for God, that we are not the creator. If a scholar is not enlightened with the faith that God is the Creator, that scholar cannot understand how or why things came into being. What we search for and what we do with our knowledge is important. After we have stored up knowledge, we then have to make a leap to a higher form of knowledge called wisdom, which involves love. We will also pray for knowledge of God. This search is undertaken only in the light of love. Write down what you think about knowledge and wisdom, and then seek only wisdom in the light of the Holy Spirit.

My Journal

- Let's listen to the children who want us to stop domestic and verbal violence, who want us to read with them rather than sitting them in front of the television. Start by going to a library or bookstore and watch your children take books off the shelves. Which story will you read with your child tonight?

- Imagine that God our Father would beam and show us love for our acts of kindness. They will ripple out into the universe and keep touching people on into infinity. What kindness did you do for someone today?

- Write down what you think about knowledge and wisdom, then seek only wisdom in the light of the Holy Spirit.

*The light shines
in the darkness.*

JOHN 1:5

Letters We Meant to Write

What letters would you write to your family, loved ones, and friends if this day or this week were your last? What do you want to say? How do you begin? What do you give as an excuse for writing after "all these years"? How you begin might be as simple as "I remember we met a long time ago when we were in the spring of our lives, and then we went separate ways. I want you to know you are important in my life, and I am thankful to have you for a friend." I remember when my friend was dying, and I took her to buy cards to say thank you to her friends. She could not write very much, but she wrote a few words to certain persons to express how special they were to her. Those little cards helped them understand they were treasured as warm hands she had held at some point in her life. Maybe when they hold the letter she wrote that day, they'll remember her warm hands and her friendship.

Life

Keep a log for a week and write down every time you say "I'll do it when…" "Wait until…" "I'll be happy when…." Be sure to note what caused you to use the word "until" or "when." You might think these are a lot of phrases to watch for, but in doing this exercise, you may notice a pattern. Each of the phrases is a flashing light that signals us to stop and stand still. Using examples from an earlier reflection, consider the effect if, when the angel Gabriel told Mary she would have a son, Mary had said, "No, I won't do it until I know man." Life as we know it would have been tremendously altered right there. But Mary didn't hesitate, and so we can continue. If Jesus had said, "No, mother, I won't do it until they bring the water jars and ask me for help," we would not have had the miracle at Cana. Imagine if Jesus had said, "I won't go to the desert until I pack some food. I'll start preaching when John gathers a good following of disciples." Or worse yet, "I won't go to Jerusalem until the authorities are willing to accept what I teach." Notice the use of the words "until" and "when." They put up obstacles and could have changed the course of history.

Now for a moment picture life as a dance. Our soul and body begin to dance when they meet, and our excuses of until or when might prevent them from dancing. Do we want to stop the dancing? Live life and expect nothing except adventure. Accept what happens, and invent new scenarios. If things don't go the way you like, change things, change your attitude, or invent new dance steps. No chains can hold us back except those we make. Plant seeds and ask someone to dance with you in the flowers.

Light

For those of us who live near cities it is sometimes hard to imagine what it must be like in the darkness. Ambient light can make midnight seem like daytime. But it must have been very dark before

God separated light from darkness "in the beginning." John's gospel describes Jesus as the light that shines to change darkness, but sometimes darkness does not accept the light. "The light shines in the darkness, and the darkness did not overcome it" (John 1:5). Jesus revealed himself as the light that came to dispel the darkness, and he makes it very easy for us to stay in the light.

Describing the transfiguration, when Jesus revealed his light and glory to three disciples, Matthew wrote, "His face shone like the sun, and his clothes became dazzling white" (17:2). The kingdom of light is ours, and God asks us to share it with others. If you know someone who lives in darkness, be a beacon, and pray that your friend will find the light.

Love

Touch the little fist of a newborn baby's hand, and feel the baby's hand close on your finger in childlike trust. This baby who has known nothing except softness and muted music in the womb has no fear, no deceit, and no hatred. Now, outside the womb, the baby needs love and gentleness and will need it for the rest of life. What about these same needs in the adults we encounter every day? Let us assume for a moment that we are having trouble with Jesus' command to love one another. We've had painful experiences with different persons, and we harbor ill feelings, like little boats tied up in our hearts. Jesus taught that he would dwell in us, but he can't find a place to tie up because of all those ill-will boats crowding our heart.

An expert in the law questioned Jesus about love and asked, "Who is my neighbor?" In answer Jesus told a story. A priest and a Levite walking from Jerusalem to Jericho passed by an injured man lying in the road. However, a Samaritan, an enemy of the Jewish people, stopped, cared for the man, and walked, while his donkey carried the injured man to an inn. The Samaritan paid for the man's lodging and care. When Jesus finished the story, he asked the expert,

"Which of these three, do you think, was a neighbor to the man who fell into the hands of the robbers?" The expert in the law replied, "The one who showed him mercy." Jesus told him, "Go and do likewise" (Luke 10:25–37).

Just in case we didn't catch Jesus' message, he repeated his lesson with his actions. Jesus was never too busy to stop, look at a person, and ask, "What do you want me to do for you?" Imagine what Jesus must have been thinking as he walked up to Jerusalem, knowing he would be tortured, beaten, mocked, crucified, and laid unceremoniously in an unmarked grave. But when he heard a man by the side of the road beg, "Son of David, have mercy on me," he stopped for him. Jesus forgot his own concerns and mental anguish. He looked into the man's unseeing eyes and asked, "What do you want me to do for you?" (Luke 18:39–41). Jesus taught us a lesson about love, and, leaving no questions about the issue, he made it clear that he desires love. Once we untie all those little ill-will boats and make room in our hearts, and then ask Jesus to move in, he will cure us of whatever is less than love. He was looking for just this when he told us to love one another. We will fall in love with the most glorious person who ever lived.

My Journal

- Keep a log for a week and write down every time you say "I'll do it when…" "Wait until…" "I'll be happy when…." Be sure to note what caused you to use the word "until" or "when."

- If you know someone who lives in darkness, be a beacon, and pray that your friend will find the light. For whom can you be a light?

- Once we make room in our hearts and ask Jesus to move in, he will cure us of whatever is less than love. What do you need to do to make more room in your heart for Jesus and others?

Mary said, "Do whatever he tells you."

JOHN 2:1–5

Mary

Mary, the mother of God, is the model for frightened young women who trust God no matter what other people say or do. She is an example for the young wed or unwed mother who despite fear and panic carries her child, and who, later on, sits worried at the same child's bedside during times of illness. Mary is often shown in paintings with the toddler Jesus playing with her veil or hair. Many artists show Mary as regal and Jesus as a tiny king, but look closely. She is holding him in her arms or on her knee as any mother would. Mary walked the Way of the Cross and stood at the foot of the cross. Michelangelo's Pieta shows Mary holding her dead son. Full of grief she bears his body across her lap. In the Pieta, Michelangelo sculpted a woman with a very strong arm supporting her son's weight. Many people believe they, too, can be comforted there in Mary's sturdy arms, and that this mother has the strength and the love to hold us all.

Mary is the model of a woman who persists in prayer. The miracle at Cana occurred because Mary persisted, despite her son's protests that the time had not come to start his ministry. She prodded him, "They have no wine." And Jesus said to her, "Woman, what concern is that to you and to me? My hour has not yet come." His mother said to the servants, "Do whatever he tells you" (John 2:1–5).

Mary, the model of perseverance, will pray for us even when we forget to pray or put it off. As a servant of God, Mary said "yes" and became the mother of a child who belonged to God, whom she did not understand. Mary watched her child die, but, understanding only as a human can, she trusted God and waited for the resurrection. Turn to her when you must stand beneath a cross and suffer something you can't understand.

Mother

What image does the word "mother" evoke? Close your eyes and picture a mother, your mother. You may see her wiping flour off her hands as she turns to look at you with the discerning look that mothers have, asking, "What did you do now?" You may picture her turning from her cooking and waving a wooden spoon. "You better get busy and study; money doesn't grow on trees, and you will need a good job!" For others, she is a working mother, doing her best to raise her family on her own.

You learned how to stand up straight when you walk. She fussed at what you wore and the music you listened to. She had her hand out for the report card and she asked, "Did you brush your teeth?" From your mother perhaps you learned that mothers have strong fingers, they know everything, and they have eagle eyes!

My mother prays for me and believes in me. She is always saying about my new schemes, "Maybe, well, yes, I think you can do that." She shows me off when I visit, and she is not ashamed to call and ask me to contribute prizes to the latest luncheon she is organizing for charity. And she always says "I love you" when I call her. She is small now, much smaller than I am, and she seems frail. Her arthritis hurts, and sometimes she seems to "go away" to another place. She is stubborn, and we struggle with our disagreements. She insists on living independently, and I think she needs to live near me and receive care. I see my handwriting in her handwritten notes; my thumb looks just like her thumb; my laugh is like hers, and the photo of her shows me what a beautiful woman she has been in my present and in my past.

Mothers have different qualities and talents, virtues and faults. You may have had a good experience of growing up, or an unsettled or even painful one. But whether you felt it or not, the predominant quality of almost every mom is love. Where did you go on this visit back to mother? How has your appreciation of her grown?

Music

Music accompanies us for most of the moments of our lives. At work, as we sip breakfast coffee, we find ourselves humming a tune we heard as we drove to work, or from our child's pull toy, or even the annoying jingle from a television commercial. Music played at weddings is very personal to the bride and groom. Brides spend a lot of time choosing the music to play while the guests are being seated, as the bridesmaids process in, when the bride "enters," during the wedding liturgy itself, and as the bride and groom walk out of the church.

The songs we choose for occasions or relaxing moments often tell a story about us. For example, the choice of wedding songs may reflect our belief in the sacredness and enduring quality of marriage. The theme from *Romeo and Juliet* was most appropriate for the mood at my wedding, since I felt my "sailor boy" was not well loved by my family and I was looking for "a place for us." My friend chose "The Rose" by Bette Midler for her wedding celebration. The wedding celebration followed bruising confrontations, and her theme song was the music that comforted and helped her get through the conflicts. If you are married, what music accompanied your wedding? Why did you choose the music you did? What music would you choose to mark your renewal of marriage vows?

Music can voice our praise of God and our thanksgiving. The action of the Holy Spirit may cause us to nod yes in response to the music or lyrics that touch our hearts and tell us that what we believe is true.

My Journal

- How do you picture Mary? What part does she play in your spiritual journey?

- How has your appreciation of your mother and mothers in general grown?

- Take some time to begin a list of music that has touched you, and explain why they are favorites. What are the lasting messages this music has for you?

Jesus said,
"Love your neighbor."

MATTHEW 5:44

Neighbor

I have been blessed to move into a neighborhood with no fences across the backyards except one neighbor who takes care of dogs. Even the gate to that yard opens into mine. If I need to find someone, I look first in my yard, then I start crossing the backyards. Usually I find a group of people leaning against a group of trees, talking, advising one another, and discussing what's new in town. If I go out to enjoy the sunset, I will not be alone for long. Someone will come by to sit and chat. During sunsets we've had thoughtful discussions about the Bible, infinity, child rearing, and teenage angst. This book has been shaped with the support of my neighbors' advice. The phrase "Come and sit for a while" is practiced among us.

Who is my neighbor is not a question. Jesus gave us a strategy for neighborliness that we can't ignore: "Love your neighbor" (Matthew 5:44). Would you rather come home late at night and be afraid, or come home late at night and be told by a neighbor the next day, "I kept a watch on your house because I knew you were late."

No

"No" is a shaking of our head, a thumbs down, a scowl, a negative word, or an angry tone of voice. The word "no" can have positive or negative effects, whether on the personal or social level. On the one hand, a "no" together with our refusal to believe something we cannot see can rock someone's world and bring dreams crashing to the ground. With our "no," we may refuse love to someone who needs us desperately. With our "no," we may burden shoulders and spirits and deflate balloons. With our "no," we may give voice to anger and teach our children to express anger destructively. We can burn piles of books, destroy buildings with a shake of our head or with a simple "no." We have so much power!

On the other hand, used properly, "no" can be one of the most valuable words in the English language. A simple "no" to a teenager might move him or her to resist drugs, cheating, lying, or other hurtful behavior. While describing the wording of the Ten Commandments as they might have been originally given to the people, Thomas Cahill (*The Gifts of the Jews*) suggests they were one negative word each: "a verb in the imperative form preceded by a negative prefix of one syllable…utterly primitive, basic injunctions on the order of 'No-kill, No-steal, No-lie.' These Ten Words [would be] easily memorized by even the simplest nomad." The wording is basic as the people were basic, very simple and very clear.

The word "no" sets boundaries that can save lives and protect those who can't take care of themselves. We all need boundaries. We need to say "no" when we mean "I don't want to do that; it's not good for you or for me."

Numbers

What's your ZIP code? Social Security number? Phone number? Medicare number? Cell phone number? Employee number? How much money do you make? How much does your medical insurance cost? How many pairs of shoes do you own? How many books do you have? These are all just numbers, aren't they? The next time someone looks up from the scanner at a store register and asks you for a number, try smiling and answering, "What a lovely day! How are you?" You might be met with a curious glance, but we need to get away from the numbers, from thinking of ourselves, others, and life as numbers. What a difference it will make to identify and focus on what is important in our lives—not how many or how much, but how blessed we are. "I have enough; whatever I have is God's gift, and it is enough."

Try a numbers exercise with your family. Make a list of how many things you have, such as jeans, shoes, socks, sweaters, books, marking pens, meals or snacks we eat every day, televisions in the house, and so on. You can count these material blessings. Really look at the list, and then think of the story of the Hebrew people walking through the desert, grumbling and complaining about what they didn't have. God gave them everything they needed, yet they wanted more. Remember this exercise and look at the list with all those possessions and gifts the next time you groan about something you think you don't have enough of. Replace the griping with thanks to God for what you have, and keep on walking!

My Journal

- How do you use "no": to help or to hurt? Be specific.

- With your family, make at least a partial list of the things you have and copy it into your journal. At least once a week, look at the list and thank God for his blessings.

*Your attitude should be
the same as that
of Christ Jesus.*

PHILIPPIANS 2:5

Obedience

"I don't want to be good! I don't know how to be good! I don't think I can be good, so forget it!" I stamped my foot, small, willful child that I was, but so wanting, so hungry, and so afraid to be alone.

"Why are you doing this to me? Why are you breaking my heart?" A grown woman shouted this, not a small child. I stood before a statue of Saint Theresa in the Carmelite monastery at Haifa in Israel. That day, as an adult moved to great distress by the war in my heart, I was arguing obedience or death with God and Saint Theresa. Yes, death is a choice we can argue about and even choose. My act of turning my back on God after I felt his touch in the Holy Land seemed to be "the last straw," and it was my decision to turn away from salvation. That's the way I saw it. God runs to meet us every day of our lives until we return in repentance, but I believed this was "it." "We've passed the point of no return and there's no turning back." So I turned to God amidst torrents of fearful tears at the next stop of the pilgrimage, in Nazareth, and I have been learn-

63

ing about obedience ever since. Our gentle God holds my hand on the long and rocky journey toward humility and obedience.

I told Saint Theresa that day, "I don't know how to be good!" What I really should have said is, "I don't want to be good and I don't want to love my neighbor." One who professes to love and follow Jesus must accept his supreme rule to "love one another." Instead, "I'm only human!" is an excuse voiced by many wayward Christians. Knowing the reality of our humanity, the apostle Paul wrote that our spiritual immaturity lies at the root of our resistance to the humble yoke of Jesus. The author of the Letter to the Hebrews wrote that his readers need to grow in faith and maturity. "About this we have much to say that is hard to explain, since you have become dull in understanding. For though by this time you ought to be teachers, you need someone to teach you again the basic elements of the oracles of God. You need milk, not solid food; for everyone who lives on milk, being still an infant, is unskilled in the word of righteousness. But solid food is for the mature, for those whose faculties have been trained by practice to distinguish good from evil" (5:11–14).

Paul urges us to work on our attitude: "Do nothing from selfish ambition or conceit, but in humility regard others as better than yourselves. Let each of you look not to your own interests, but to the interests of others. Let the same mind be in you that was in Christ Jesus" (Philippians 2:3–5).

Christ's attitude was characterized by perfect obedience to God our Father, even to emptying himself, "adopting the condition of a slave" (Philippians 2:7). Jesus taught us that when we accept obedience to God, it is not a burden of slavery but the acceptance of the mantle and gentle yoke of the Son of God. This means conforming our will to divine authority, with trust that God's rule guides us to an abundant life. The opposite of an attitude of obedience is hardening our hearts, refusing to listen to God's teaching and complaining that we are someplace we don't want to be. Hebrews says that disobedience kept the Israelites wandering in the desert, and repeats the thought from Psalm 95: "O that today you would listen to his voice! Do not harden your hearts" (verses 7–8).

We know when we're being disobedient. Learning obedience isn't easy. We trudge through the desert of stubbornness, complaining and whimpering. We have to remind ourselves to pray, and whisper the line of a hymn, "Abba, Father, you are the potter, I am the clay." With this hymn we place our whole being in the hands of the Father, and ask God to "mold us…into the image of Jesus your Son." Think to yourself, "Make me good," and God will mold us.

Several of us in a Bible study group pointed out that we didn't like reading the book of Numbers because the old story did not apply to us. However, believing we can find a lesson in all of God's word in Scripture, we kept reading. My friend Kathy advised us, "We could use a lesson in obedience. God means business, and we are all looking forward to the promised land. From Numbers I learned that God means what he says, and that God's commands are not requests. God doesn't just make suggestions that we may ignore. Our Creator has something wonderful in store for us. Let us continue our study of the word so we can continue to learn from the mistakes the Israelites made in the desert. Let us trust our Lord so that we are not left in the wilderness any longer than we need to be." May your prayer help you to find your way out whenever you are lost in the wilderness of disobedience and bring you to a wonderful place of peace!

My Journal

- Think and write about some instances when you accepted God's will, even though it was difficult. Also, write about instances when you resisted, how you felt, what happened, and so on.

*Jesus said,
"Your Father knows
what you need
before you ask him."*

MATTHEW 6:8

Prayer

Telly Savalas used to play a television character named Kojak who would ask, "Who loves ya, baby?" Well, search for our true lover as we will, we finally come to realize that God is the one who loves us the most—eternally and unconditionally—who watches over us every minute, and who knows our soul intimately. But if we neglect to turn to God in prayer, we might discover a deep gap opening between God and us. The book of Judges describes the chasm that developed between God and Israel after the Hebrew people entered the Promised Land. The people worshiped the way they wanted, and they manipulated the law of God to fit their personal needs and beliefs. "In those days there was no king in Israel, all the people did what was right in their own eyes" (21:25). Like the people of Israel in the time of the Judges, during my youth I sought a belief that I found comfortable. If I went to church, I would pray and weep: "Save me from anxiety," but I was not saved from anxiety. I would read St. Francis' prayer, "Make me an instrument of your peace," but

I was not peaceful. Despite my spiritual loneliness, I would not listen to God. I could not realize that God would remove my anxiety and give me peace. First, I had to turn to God and learn to pray.

Seeing their Teacher go off to pray, the disciples asked Jesus to teach them how to pray. Jesus answered, "Go into your room and shut the door and pray to your Father who is in secret." Jesus taught the disciples to call on God for daily bread, forgiveness, and protection from "the evil one" (Matthew 6:5–21; Luke 11:1–4). Once I heard a woman praying "Our Father…thy will be done, on earth, as it is in heaven." She placed great emphasis on "Thy will be done," and I became aware that I need to learn to turn my will over to our Father. I began to pray, "Thy will be done; help me pray every day. Help me remember to pray. I cannot do this alone."

We need to form the habit of prayer at the beginning of our prayer journey. Setting a routine can assist us in focusing. As we begin to pray, we can picture Jesus holding our hand and walking with us. Ask Jesus to lead us to our Father.

Let's be grateful to God who fills us with gifts of grace. God loves us so much that estrangement from him is darkness and pain. Our loving God will deliver us from anxiety, and his powerful yet gentle love can transform us. We cannot earn God's love; we can only respond to it with the humility of a child. When we ask, "What do you want from me, God?" we might find the answer as simple as this: "Spend some time with me, and know that I love you."

Presence of God

When my husband and I went traveling, I used to accuse him of hurtling through some of the most beautiful countryside in Europe and Ireland. "Wait," I'd shout over the wind, "look at that stone!" He would look at me as though I were some kind of wild woman, but he would bring the car to a stop. Then I'd rush out and sneak stealthily through a herd of cows to touch an ancient stone. "Maybe the Druids put this here," we would murmur, musing over the mystery of a long-ago civilization. I caressed the stone and stepped back into the car.

Do we sometimes hurtle through life, doing what others want us to do? Do we schedule in time for stopping to touch old mysterious stones, watch beautiful children, enjoy purple-blue iris flowers, or feel the wind blowing on our faces? Do we stop to think about the presence of God everywhere around us? Take a child outside and sit down, or if it is a small child, run around after the child! Watch the child touch everything and share his joy at flowers, fur caught in a bush, clouds, little piles of dirt, empty bird's nests. Each thing moves through the world and has now come to rest in or over your yard. Express your joy and proclaim the wonder of God! God is here. God is everywhere. Stop and acknowledge the creative presence of God and feel the wind whisper, "Be still and know that I am God!"

Problems and Pain

In the Letter to the Philippians, Paul challenges us to exchange fear and worry for the peace that only God can give, even while we are in pain. If we do not believe this, we will concentrate only on our pain, fear, heartache, disillusionment, and despair. Rather than moan about being in prison, Paul sang with joy about God's love. "Rejoice in the Lord always; again I will say, Rejoice!…Do not worry about anything, but in everything by prayer and supplication with thanksgiving let your requests be made known to God. And the peace of God, which surpasses all understanding, will guard your hearts and your minds in Christ Jesus" (4:4–7). There are two great promises in Philippians, "I can do all things through him who strengthens me" and "My God will fully satisfy every need of yours according to his riches in glory in Christ Jesus" (4:13, 19). Read these lines when you think you have a problem or have a heavy heart. Enjoy the thought of the relief and riches God will give you!

My Journal

- Is prayer an important part of your life? How?

- Does your schedule allow time for stopping to touch old mysterious stones, watch beautiful children, enjoy purple-blue iris flowers, or feel the wind blowing on your face? Do you stop to think about the presence of God everywhere around you? Write about some of these experiences.

*God created humankind
in his image.*

GENESIS 1:27

Quality

Have you ever received a recall on an automobile or a piece of baby furniture or other manufactured product? Improvements in technology have enhanced our ability to change sophisticated goods rapidly. Companies have the ability to give us new and improved products very quickly, creating what we call "throw away technology." Do you ever wonder why craftsmanship became unimportant and too expensive? Do you hunger for quality? When I worked for AT&T, I was astounded that we needed Quality Teams and Quality Assurance committees. Products were rushed to market, and if problems were encountered, chronics teams were assembled, and the customers with troubles were assigned to a queue to be addressed ahead of "routine" troubles. Software products were patched, and if problems couldn't be quickly fixed, products were recalled.

Once I found a cane rocking chair on a trash pile. The seat had a big hole in it from a lot of use, and perhaps someone had stood on the seat. I saw the potential beauty of the rocker and wanted to repair it. After searching, I found a person who could fix a hand-caned chair. When I brought the chair to him, he ran his hands over it. "Ah! A mother's rocker!" he said. "It's been abused, but it is a fine piece of wood. Is it oak?" he asked.

I shrugged. "I don't know."

"What color is it?" he asked. Then I found out that the only man who could fix my broken, hand-caned rocker was blind. I watched him move his fingers over the wood of the chair and diagnose other problems the rocker had. "It will need a little mending here." He pointed to a break in the wood. Here was a true craftsman who lovingly handled a work of art. I understood that day what quality is. He fixed a broken chair that someone had thrown on a trash pile. I will never forget the care he showed as he restored the beautiful handmade chair.

Many persons have painted or sculpted the hands of God in the act of creation, as if fascinated by the "hands-on" attitude of a loving Creator. God lifts us up and runs his loving hands over us. "Ah! It is good." In us God recognizes his handiwork, his image, even if badly treated and abused, and he molds us with his hands. Then—and it has to be because the Creator recognizes good quality underneath all our grime—those loving hands continue to raise us up each time our own actions land us in the dirt again.

My Journal

- When have you admired the beauty of a piece of art or music or an aspect of nature? Describe it.

- How have you experienced being re-formed by God?

Jesus said,
"Everyone who hears
these words of mine
and acts on them
will be like a wise man
who built his house on rock."

Matthew 7:24

Responsibility

In a file full of articles on responsibility, I found a writing exercise I did twenty years ago. On one sheet I wrote: "Recovery is based on the premise that I am responsible for myself. I will devote myself to learning one new behavior: I will take care of myself. How do I feel about that?" The exercise was inspired by a book called *Co-dependent No More.* To oversimplify, a co-dependent person supports another's behavior and accepts ownership and responsibility for the other's behavior. The book challenges the co-dependent person to change and take responsibility only for personal behavior.

I grew up feeling sorry for things I did that I never should have felt sorry for, worrying if anyone would love me, apologizing for the way I looked and the way I did things, and trying to hide what I perceived as my weaknesses. In the writing exercise I reflected, "I want to change because I feel unhappy, and I allow things I cannot control to make me unhappy." I needed to "get in control," but now I see that the problem with what I wrote is the word "control."

If we delve into our hearts and think about one thing that keeps us from living a full Christian life, we often find that it concerns our sense of responsibility. If we believe we have to control things, we are unhappy because we can't shape events, and we recognize how much we try to control God. We need to understand, accept, and discern what it is we are trying to control.

Jesus tells us, "Wait, listen, and pray!" Jesus says "wait" about 135 times a day. A friend wrote to me: "Waiting on God is impossible for me also. I think I am getting more patient the older I get, but sometimes I am just not sure. He tells us to 'be still and know that I am God.' Let's give it a try today." With this attitude of waiting on God and with a lot of prayer, we can hand control over to God, who has all the controls anyway. What we are doing is claiming the peace that Christ gave when he said, "Peace be with you, my peace I give to you." When he lived among us, did Jesus ever try to take control or question what his own responsibility was?

We can rewrite the exercise I spoke of: "It is my responsibility to learn one new behavior. That behavior will be to love God and my neighbor. I will pray for patience." That's it; we can't control the events of our lives or the lives of others. We are responsible to love and protect the young, the unable, and widows. We will be gentle with little ones and teach them love for God and for others. We will show our joy at being children of God and kneel at the feet of God in adoration, with humility, thanks, and praise. Our responsibility is to wait on the word God speaks to us. What are your major responsibilities?

Retreats

What is it about our lives that keeps getting in the way of peace and quiet, of time for reflective prayer? We may try to get away to make a retreat but discover that what's getting in the way of our life is life itself. Jesus did not make a retreat in a monastery, but he did go away alone—into the desert, up a mountain—to renew his relationship with God and listen to God's voice. We have to take time to pray in quiet, since that is when we can hear the voice of God, counseling us and telling us we are loved and valued for what we are and do.

The prophet Elijah ran away when Jezebel threatened to kill him after he killed the prophets of Baal. He was afraid, burned out, and fed up with his "career" as a prophet of God. He asked God to let him die. Instead, God sent Elijah to Horeb, the mountain of God, for a forty-day solitary retreat. On the mountain, the Lord listened to Elijah's complaints and prayers, then assigned Elijah new duties including selecting Elisha to be his assistant (1 Kings 19:3–17). When we have reached the end of our rope, beleaguered and in pain, how appealing it sounds to go on a forty-day retreat to meditate and pray. However, we're rarely able to take that much time away, so perhaps we can make our own retreat.

My friends Charlie and Kathy get up early in the morning to read Scripture. Picturing them sitting with a cup of coffee as the sun rises always gets me back on track. I do not need extra sleep as much as I need that extra half-hour of quiet retreat. There is something holy about the sunrise and sunset hours. Nature seems so quiet, as if aware something wonderful is happening. We might not be able to make a forty-day retreat, but we could take one hour each day at sunrise or sunset. In 365 days, that hour a day adds up to about seven days of retreat.

Begin your retreat time with God by doing as Jesus did. Find a solitary place, be quiet, listen. If you hear only bird song and crickets, listen. If a cat comes by, pet her. The Lord may want you to hear a beautiful song and touch something soft. This might well lead to an appreciation of the beauty of creation. May God bless your retreat hours with his graceful presence.

Rules

My friend Mike tells me the number one rule is "Be kind." My friend Bill tells me that in his home he put up a chalkboard shared by his wife, two daughters, and grandmother. He wrote "Rules" and said the first one was "Be nice to one another." He went on to say that life is a circle. At the center of the circle is truth. The farther you get from the center, the farther you are from the value of truth. Rule number two is: Stay in the center of the circle.

The Letters to Timothy include rules to Timothy, the bishop of Ephesus, because God's work is done best by exercising discipline. "If I am delayed, you may know how one ought to behave in the household of God, which is the church of the living God, the pillar and bulwark of the truth" (1 Timothy 3:15). One of the first things I do in religion class is to bring the learners into church and teach them how to conduct themselves. They learn how to use the books of prayers and songs usually provided in churches; how to show respect for God and others (which generally leads to a discussion of why they deserve respect). Finally, we discuss the importance and benefits of participating in the Eucharist and other sacraments, such as reconciliation. We all need to remember that the house of God is a holy place where respect, honor, and reverence are not mere suggestions but a sign of our love for God.

My Journal

- Rewrite this exercise: "It is my responsibility to learn one new behavior." What are your major responsibilities?

- How and when do you (or will you) make time for longer periods of quiet prayer? Journaling is an excellent starting point.

Jesus said, "Be perfect as your heavenly Father is perfect."

MATTHEW 5:48

Saint

In the book of Revelation, John describes the angels of God putting a seal on the foreheads of "a great multitude that no one could count...standing before the throne and before the Lamb, robed in white, with palm branches in their hands...singing, 'Amen! Blessing and glory and wisdom and thanksgiving and honor and power and might be to our God forever and ever!'" (Revelation 7:3, 9–12). This great multitude is the saints, and wouldn't we love to be among them one day? Jesus said, "Be perfect as your heavenly Father is perfect" (Matthew 5:48)—but how? Depend on God to show us the way and to enable us to follow it. God does this through Jesus.

According to Paul, "those whom he foreknew he also predestined to be conformed to the image of his Son....And those whom he predestined he also called; and those whom he called he also justified; and those whom he justified he also glorified" (Romans 8:29–30).

This knowledge makes me want to dance to these words from the Letter of John: "See what love the Father has given us, that we should be called children of God; and that is what we are" (1 John 3:1).

Saints are the sanctified children of God, and God has selected us to be his children. Claim the promise of being a child of God and have confidence in God's promises. Saints have this confidence and live accordingly. To sustain us in our journey, we know that Jesus prays for us as he calls us to love and trust in God's plan. While we are on the same journey the saints walked, the steps we take are our own individual steps. We can't walk in the saints' footsteps or do things the same way they did, but we can pray for their help! Choose a great saint as a model, mentor, and companion in prayer. Today the saints, who knew human tribulations and human weakness, enjoy God's intimate embrace. God has blessed us as he blessed them.

Satan

We humans have many ways of depicting Satan. One day when I was discussing temptation with a minister, he suggested I say, "Go to hell, Satan!" This is similar to what Jesus said to the devil in the desert, "Away with you, Satan!" (Matthew 2:10). To describe the network of hate Satan builds up against God and the lengths he will go to win over God's creation, C.S. Lewis wrote a book called *The Screwtape Letters.* A "veteran" devil named Screwtape writes to his nephew, Wormwood, training him to be a better devil and teaching him persistence in the war to convert Christians to Satan. Screwtape describes humans as wavering between falling into sin and returning to God: "Their nearest approach to constancy therefore is undulation—the repeated return to a level from which they repeatedly fall back, a series of troughs and peaks."

We've all experienced troughs of numbness and dryness. Screwtape comments that "some of [God's] special favorites have gone through longer and deeper troughs than anyone else....If only the will to walk is really there [God] is pleased even with their stumbles."

Lewis describes being under Satan's power as having one's eyes closed and scabbed over. Jesus described persons in this state as "those who have eyes but cannot see."

When the soul of the new Christian turns to God, Satan loses. Lewis depicts the reaction in hell (the Kingdom of Noise) by putting these words into Screwtape's mouth. "You have let a soul slip through your fingers....It makes me mad to think about it."

When we turn to God, God takes off the wet clinging garment of sin and gives us fresh white clothes. The new Christians recognize the ones who helped and supported them against sin as a "network" of angels. How many times has your guardian angel played a part in protecting you against Satan?

Suffering

Suffering is a state of pain and anguish, and we often can't do anything except endure it. A friend once told me, "You endure pain and you persevere in your faith. Should I wail and throw my arms all around? What good would that do except to raise my anxiety level and make me hurt more? Yes, suffering hurts, but if I quiet my mind and pray, the suffering diminishes. It is as if God were bearing some of the pain for me."

In the Letter to Hebrews we are advised to fix our eyes on Jesus as a running mate who will help us. "Let us run with perseverance the race that is set before us, looking to Jesus the pioneer and perfecter of our faith, who for the sake of the joy that was set before him endured the cross" (12:1–2). We try to understand God's plan when we suffer, when the world of pain collides with the unknown world of release and resurrection. We know that Jesus said the life of one who follows him would be accompanied with fire and pain, but like Paul, we ask God to relieve the suffering (2 Corinthians 12:7–9).

One benefit of suffering is that it builds character, and we wonder what that means. Paul explains: "We also boast in our sufferings, knowing that suffering produces endurance, and endurance produces character, and character produces hope" (Romans 5:3–4). If we persevere in our suffering and accept God's plan with faith, then peace will envelop us in the form of "character."

Someday when we see God's face, we will understand that the power of God's love protects us. Paul offers the balm of faith for those who suffer. "We do not lose heart. For our light and momentary troubles are achieving for us an eternal glory that far outweighs them all" (2 Corinthians 4:16–17).

Sunset

Although we have to look away from the intensity of the setting sun to avoid damaging our eyes, our gaze constantly returns to the sky. Is our attention caught by colors that we don't see during the day? Pink, coral, salmon, and gold tinge the sky, and small clouds turn from pink to rose with gold linings. Glints and gleams touch ordinary objects with light that startles us.

In the same way, glints and gleams of the inspiration of the Holy Spirit touch our ordinary work, turning our humble efforts into meaningful deeds. In a sunset, the sun sinks in splendor, repeating a promise like one Jesus left with us: "I am with you always." This promise is fulfilled every morning, at every Eucharist, and at every birth and death. Reflecting on all this, a friend of mine says she looks at sunsets "in a different light" now. We sit quietly together lost in our own thoughts and watch God's splendor bathe our world with a hint of the glory and grandeur of God. Together we silently thank God.

My Journal

- Claim the promise of being a child of God. How will you do this?

- How many times has your guardian angel played a part in protecting you against Satan?

- Choose one of the passages from Paul on suffering, and write your reflections on it.

*Rekindle the gift of God
which is within you.*

2 TIMOTHY 1:6

Talents

Do you remember the parable of the talents? A man gave talents to his servants. The first two servants invested their talents, made more, and gained rewards from the master. A third man buried his talent because he was afraid to risk the talent he was given, or maybe he did not feel he had "enough." Returning only the one talent his master gave him, he was chastised and punished for hiding his talent and not doing anything with it (Matthew 25:14–30). In the context of the parable, the Greek word *talanton* means a great deal of money, about two years' wages. It is the source of the English word "talent" or natural ability.

In his gospel, Matthew follows the parable of the talents with a description of what Jesus might say to us at the Last Judgment. "I was hungry and you gave me food, I was thirsty and you gave me something to drink, I was a stranger and you welcomed me, I was naked and you gave me clothing, I was sick and you took care of me, I was in prison and you visited me....Truly I tell you, just as you did

81

it to one of the least of these who are members of my family, you did it to me" (Matthew 25:34–40). If we keep our hands in our pockets, that is, unwilling to share our time, talents, and treasures with others, we are like the man who hid his talent for fear of losing it.

Make a list of the things you do well and that you love to do. Consider that these talents are gifts from the Lord. Without the gifts and blessings of the Holy Spirit, we would not be able to speak or write well, to sing or draw or dance, to teach or perform life-saving surgery, or to do the many other wonderful things human beings do. Write how you will use and share your talents to glorify God.

Thanksgiving

At least once a year, during the American celebration of Thanksgiving Day, we have the chance to say we are thankful. We express our thanks that a tiny group of freedom-seeking immigrants left their homes and faced starvation, storms, and cold. We whisper thanks to the little group and we turn to thank God for our blessings.

Thank God for snow and warm beaches, for memories, for grandparents, babies, kittens, and puppies. List your cold things, warm things, old things, and new things. Thank God for families who love us. Thank God for sunny days so you can feel the warmth of the sun on your face.

Thank God for sidewalks, green lawns, and flower gardens. As teenagers zoom by with their new driving permits, offer a prayer for their safety. Thank God for stop signs, speed zones, police officers, and safety instructors. We stop and watch the school children, burdened with back packs, running to meet their parents. And we thank God for their healthy, inquisitive minds, for the hope of the future, and for their teachers who teach five to six lessons a day and are concerned for their students, who stay up late at night assessing students' work and preparing class plans.

Thank God for the special talents he has given you. Thank God for your freedom and health, for the possessions you have.

Thanking God moves us to stop and write a special Thanksgiving prayer. "Father, all-powerful and loving God, your gifts are countless; your goodness is infinite. On Thanksgiving Day we express our gratitude for your goodness and love. Fill our hearts with concern and love for our fellow men, women, and children so we may share your gifts in loving service." A prayer of thanksgiving can open our hearts to the beauty of the world, and lift our spirits and our mental attitude. A prayer of thanksgiving for blessings can bring the joy of God's gifts to the forefront of our minds and touch our hearts.

Make a list of God's blessings. Start with the people of God who inspire and motivate you. Go next to the gifts of nature, the rainbows and the breezes. Think of the foods you love to eat, the feel of ice cream on your tongue, the tang of bread and butter pickles. Think of the smells you love that stir good memories: the smell of a baby's hair after a bath, of clean sheets, of roses, of books, of the outdoors. Think of the songs that speak to you. Then write your own Thanksgiving prayer.

My Journal

- Make a list of the things you do well and that you love to do. Consider that these talents are gifts from the Lord. Write how you will use and share your talents to glorify God.

- Be aware of God's blessings. Then write your own Thanksgiving prayer.

Jesus prayed,
"May all of them be one,
Father, just as you are in me
and I am in you."

JOHN 17:21

Unity

Unity is the state of being joined together, of being one in some way. For example, the United States is fifty autonomous governing bodies joined together as one nation. We might be a contentious and fractious bunch, but our shared beliefs in justice, in the values our country is built on, and in the Constitution hold us together. We might have disputes over various matters, but when the chips are down we are a family. So, too, the Christian community is united in its belief that Jesus Christ is God, Messiah, Savior, Brother, and Lord. Differing in the way we worship God, in some of our religious beliefs, our goal is the same, to bring about the kingdom of God— a kingdom of love, justice, and peace—leading to eternal life with Jesus in heaven.

Jesus wanted all people to be with him. At the end of the Last Supper on Holy Thursday, Jesus prayed for the disciples and for those people who would come to believe in him. "He looked toward heaven and prayed: 'I ask not only on behalf of these, but also on behalf of those who will believe in me through their word, that they may all be one. As you, Father, are in me and I am in you, may they also be in us, so that the world may believe that you have sent me'" (John 17:20–21).

Imagine that unity is all of us inside a circle. Jesus, the Alpha and the Omega, the Beginning and the End, is the line encircling us. All Christians dwell in the same heart, united in a single family with one Father and one Brother (Revelation 21:6).

My Journal

- What can you do to promote unity among Christians, beginning in your own neighborhood? What steps would you take?

*Before you were born
I consecrated you.*

JEREMIAH 1:5

Values

Think of a value as something that is worthy or desirable, highly regarded and esteemed, such as a belief, precept, standard, or action, then think of the values that God cherishes in us. The Letter to the Hebrews outlines activities and values that please God, such as perseverance in following Jesus, being peacemakers, being holy, being positive and eliminating bitterness, loving one another, offering hospitality to strangers, caring for prisoners and the mistreated, honoring marriage vows, and being content with what we have. "Let us fix our eyes on Jesus....Pursue peace with everyone, and the holiness without which no one will see the Lord. See to it that no one fails to obtain the grace of God; that no root of bitterness springs up and causes trouble, and through it many become defiled....Let mutual love continue" (12:14–15; 13:1).

Living with a focus on what God values shows that we believe God has plans for us and will never leave us alone. It involves examining where we concentrate our energies. For example, we must ask if God values our intense ambition. In Scripture the word "ambition" is usually preceded by the word selfish. God values love, justice, goodness, humility, faithfulness, and loving patience.

My friend Christy challenged our Bible study group to a self-evaluation while studying John the Baptist, who said he was a small voice crying in the desert for one whose shoes he was not worthy to touch. In perfect humility, he was doing what God valued, using his passionate speaking talent to awake Israel to prepare for the Lord.

Try keeping a checklist like this one to evaluate value-driven behavior:

Am I child of God, doing what God values?

Do I live according to the commandments and beatitudes?

Do I live as Jesus lived and taught, witnessing to his values?

Do I practice the gifts the Holy Spirit has given me: "love, joy, peace, patience, kindness, generosity, faithfulness, gentleness, and self-control" (Galatians 5:22–23)?

Violence

Violence is forceful action that infringes on the rights of another person or persons. You can inflict physical violence on someone's person, rights, or property, or verbal and mental violence by infringing on someone's peace of mind with insults and threats. An important issue regarding violence is what message we are giving our children. As adults, are we letting our children get away with bad attitudes, dirty looks, and bad language, or are we consciously removing violence from our children's lives by saying no to all forms of violence in our homes? Our role is to engender peacefulness in our children. Consciously removing violence means that parents have to be in touch with the adults at the homes their children visit to ensure there are no weapons accessible. It means asking if responsible adults are always present. If it means we monitor or control the Internet sites the children visit, the video games they play, and the music they love in order to ensure that nonviolence is the message, then so be it. We can stop and replace the violent messages pouring into our children's minds with God's message of love. Discussions about the harm violent programs and games can do is an excellent approach.

Scripture teaches us that if we worship the worthless idols of aggression and violence, then we will become aggressive and violent. "They went after false idols and became false; they followed the nations that were around them, concerning whom the Lord had commanded them that they should not do as they did" (2 Kings 17:15). If we hide behind the lame excuse of preserving our children's self-esteem and look for ways to say yes when no is the only acceptable answer, if we let our children make their own decisions and live their own lives when it endangers their faith and values, then we will destroy our children's future.

Violence often erupts from unresolved conflict. We can't solve every problem, but we can work with others on the problems we have some control over. We can try to keep a peaceful vision of Jesus in our homes, creating an atmosphere of love. Imagine the Holy Spirit hovering over your home as he did in Genesis when "the Spirit of the Lord hovered over the waters." Write about the images and words that remind you of the peace that Christ offers. Bring them up when family violence, physical or mental, erupts; discuss with your children the violent images and words they encounter in their peer environment. Suggest, for example, that if they are angry, they think about Jesus' example. We all need to learn to ask for God's grace to withhold our hands from striking back, to help us control what we say, to do something nice for someone in secret, to bless those who frustrate us, and to praise someone who is discouraged. Then we will accomplish God's will for us when he sent the Spirit of Jesus to hover over us.

Vocation

Vocation is usually described as a call from God to do his work for the benefit of the community. Just as Jesus called the first disciples, imagine that he calls us to surround him, walk with him, and live according to his teaching. "Follow me, and I will make you fish for people" (Matthew 4:19; John 1:43; Mark 1:17). The disciples were a motley assortment of men and women, sinners like the rest of us. They did not know what their job was or who this man Jesus really was, but they loved him and learned to trust him. Their vocation was to become true disciples of Jesus, living and sharing his word and the bread of life, to become followers unto death for Christ.

The Old Testament records the calling of Moses and of the prophets Jeremiah, Ezekiel, and Isaiah, who believed they were unworthy and unfit to serve God, but the Lord gave them special talents to become the voice of God. Moses gave the Lord the most excuses and the Lord gave Moses the partnership of his brother Aaron to help him. In the book of Exodus we can read the excuses Moses used, which might be paraphrased, "Who are you? Oh, Lord, you couldn't mean me. I can't talk well. I am not worthy to serve you" (3:11—4:17). Isaiah was frightened that he had been chosen because he felt unworthy and unclean. "I am ruined! For I am a man of unclean lips, and I live among a people of unclean lips, and my eyes have seen the King, the Lord Almighty." The Lord cleansed Isaiah's lips and gave him the words to say (Isaiah 6:5). Jeremiah said he was too young, "I do not know how to speak, for I am only a boy," but the Lord gave Jeremiah words and promised not to leave him alone. "Do not be afraid for I am with you to deliver you" (Jeremiah 1:6, 8). God showed Ezekiel God's power in a vision, and then gave Ezekiel words to eat so he could speak the word of God.

When we hear a call, we too might feel the burden of being unworthy or unfit, and we may struggle against the call. But when we finally respond to it, our answer must be a considered, free, humble, and mature commitment to love, serve, and obey God, or we will not be able to sustain it. We must be convinced that our answer is right. Later on, when times get rough, we might have to fall back on the memory of the love we felt when we first answered, "Here I am, Lord."

When God calls, God reminds us that he has a plan for us. Jeremiah wrote that God chooses, knows, forms, and anoints us when we are still in the womb (Jeremiah 1:4–10). Through baptism, God appoints all Christians to be prophets, to witness to the Christian way. Like Jeremiah and Moses, we might make excuses about our age or inadequacy, but God always equips his chosen ones and dwells in our hearts if we choose to say yes. Can you see yourself as one of the frightened, "called" people we read about in Scripture? You are!

Overwhelmed by the beauty and majesty of God, the prophet usually protested that he couldn't do what God asked. The protest was offered out of the same fear we feel, "I don't know anything, I can't speak, I'm too young, I'm too old, I'm afraid of the cost." Imagine that God is calling you to do something you are afraid to do. It may be something totally new that you never thought about until the moment God called, or it may be something you've always wanted to do. Sometimes we talk or drink or become work-aholics to obliterate his voice, but he waits for us. He is the wall we lean on. What is your talent and vocation? How did God get your attention? Called to be a prophet, how will you speak out on God's behalf?

My Journal

- What is your vocation? How did God get your attention? Called to be a prophet, how will you speak out on God's behalf?

- Try keeping a checklist to evaluate value-driven behavior.

*The fear of the Lord
is the beginning
of knowledge.*

PROVERBS 1:7

Wisdom

Make a list of what you will take with you when you leave this earth. Just as there is a one-bag limit when we board a commercial airliner, there are limits on what we can take with us when we make our final journey. The bundles we carry as we leave earth can contain only non-material and non-mortal items. After we sift out the material and mortal, what remains in our bundles is only what is stored in our hearts and minds. We will carry our bundles when we try to pass through the narrow door that Jesus used as the image of the entry to salvation. "Strive to enter through the narrow door; for many, I tell you, will try to enter and will not be able" (Luke 13:23–24). Jesus wants us to know that the way to salvation is like a small door. If we reach the door, we will not pass through it if we are burdened with useless items. But if we spend our Christian lives seeking to fill our hearts and minds with love and wisdom, our bundles will be easy to carry.

Wisdom, the highest form of knowledge, is the quality of being quick and keen in perception, the ability to see truths unclouded by the mud of mortality. Wisdom is what we do with the knowledge we gain from prayer and study, and what abstract concepts we form with our knowledge. A gift of the Holy Spirit, wisdom is the result of our quest for a relationship with God as we try to discern the mind of God. Jesus taught the disciples, so they had knowledge; he let them witness healing miracles, the transfiguration, and the resurrection. However, they did not understand the significance of what they heard and saw until the Holy Spirit gave them the gift of wisdom. Then the disciples translated their knowledge to a higher level of truth.

We can approach the mind of God if we heed the teaching in the book of Proverbs to listen, study, treasure, and love God's word; to store up the words of the wise ones; and to respect and revere God's greatness. "If you indeed cry out for insight, and raise your voice for understanding; if you seek it like silver, and search for it as for hidden treasures—then you will understand the fear of the Lord and find the knowledge of God" (Proverbs 2:2–5, 3:5). If we pray for wisdom and discernment, the Lord will hear us.

"With child"

A long time ago people did not use the word "pregnant." A more acceptable term to describe the woman was "confined in a delicate condition." "With child" was another way to describe the woman's condition.

I like to watch a pregnant woman's hands caress her growing belly. Here I describe a woman who is "with child."

Ancient phrase, yet apt.
The woman is in awe.
Her hands stray to her belly
Soon to be full with child.
Her hands are amazed at the changes in her body.

There begins a special communication
Between a woman and her body.
"With child." She seeks to understand.
Her child, his child, God's child.
God's gift.

Do you wonder what a mother is thinking while she pats her belly?

Maybe she is saying to that belly, "Well, I'm doing it!

Heck, what am I doing? You're doing it all actually.

I made a life shattering decision to welcome you—

But actually, I think this decision was made by you and God.

To come to me.

Your daddy and I really thought we had it all together.

(Forgive me, child, that's a phrase we use for expressing our satisfaction with status quo.

We have it all…all's well; no need to change things, add nothing, delete nothing.)

Then, you came! You won't be here for a few months yet, but you are growing daily.

You have taken hold of me. You come first.

You are continuing.

You direct my every movement and decision.

You move in and take over with your needs and demands.

I can't smoke. I can't drink, except milk (which I always avoided).

Will you be soft and loving?

Will you hug me and smile?

You will roll around in the grass and blow kisses at butterflies.

You will laugh, for laughter is the essence of life.

Without laughter, we are not alive.

Will you look like your daddy? Or like me? Or like both of us?

It's up to you and God.

I'm going to take a vitamin with a glass of milk now.

Then I think I'll take a walk and think of bunnies, kittens, and little engines that could.

Worry

Worry is like an uneasy wolf that gnaws at our insides. Worry clouds our vision and keeps us from seeing the paths that are open to us. Just after the Our Father we recite at Mass, the celebrant prays that God may preserve us from sin and anxiety. Don't we believe God will protect us? We ask God to deliver us from anxiety, but we don't pay attention when God tells us not to worry! Jesus said, "Be not afraid," yet we still see wrinkled foreheads and tears on our cheeks. Jesus said, "Give me all your burdens; be like little children."

The Letter of Peter urges the persecuted Christians: "Humble yourselves therefore under the mighty hand of God, so that he may exalt you in due time. Cast all your anxiety on him, because he cares for you" (1 Peter 5:6–7). Am I afraid that God won't lift me up? Do I dare to think he cannot lift me up?

My Journal

- What will you have prepared to take with you when you leave this earth?

- When have I experienced the effect of placing my anxiety in God's hands?

*For now we see
in a mirror dimly.*

1 CORINTHIANS 13:12

Xanadu

Samuel Taylor Coleridge, an English Romantic poet, fell asleep under the influence of what might today be a cold medicine laced with a sleeping aid. He awoke with a vision and wrote "Kubla Khan" which begins, "In Xanadu did Kubla Khan / a stately pleasure-dome decree…a savage place! As holy and enchanted / As e'er beneath a waning moon was haunted / By woman wailing for her demon-lover!" His doorbell rang and he was disturbed by a caller. When he got back to work, the image was gone, and the mystical pool of imagination he had been looking into dried up. He lost the image, but the lines of poetry he wrote are often called the best visionary poetry in the English language. For that moment, he drank from the muse's cup of inspiration.

Poets may seek inspiration from Calliope, the eloquent muse of music and poetry, and often die never having met her. To be inspired is to breathe the rarified air where the muse dwells, escaping the "mortal coil" and achieving heights and realms where angels dwell and mystical secrets are revealed. It is said that John Milton reached these heights when he wrote *Paradise Lost* and Dante reached the heights when he wrote *The Divine Comedy.*

Poets, writers, and painters conjure images and sounds from their imaginations and create stories, poetry, and pictures that examine the mysteries that humans with "clay feet" hunger to know but can't clearly see. The artist looks upward and sometimes sees, as Jacob saw, a ladder with angels on it. He or she hungers for access to the ladder. The "curse" of being human is to hunger for mystical knowledge, yet see only imperfectly, "For now we see in a mirror dimly" (1 Corinthians 13:12). We try to "see" into heaven to find the wisdom we hunger for so intensely, but we can't achieve that mystical wisdom on our own. "But we speak God's wisdom, secret and hidden, which God decreed before the ages for our glory" (1 Corinthians 2:7).

To escape the "mortal coil" and become mature in our spiritual development, we must believe we can take on the mind of Christ through the power of the Holy Spirit. Paul admonishes pagans who "were enticed and led astray to idols that could not speak." No one can be inspired, "no one can say 'Jesus is Lord,' except by the Holy Spirit" (1 Corinthians 12:2–3). Like Coleridge, we try to describe Xanadu, but we must sit in silence and ask the Spirit to come into our minds and hearts, fill us with his fire, inspire us with wisdom and light, and show us visions we dream of!

Xmas

If you have you seen Christmas written as "Xmas," you may have bristled at that and sputtered "Keep Christ in Christmas!" (Look in chapter C). However, "X" is the way some cultures abbreviate the name of Christ. If you transliterated the Greek word for Christ into English it might be spelled XPIETOE. The Greek "X" in English is "Ch," RHO is "R," and Sigma (E) is "S." So people shorten Christ to

"X" and add "mas." I have even seen people write this on Christmas cards, as in "Happy Xmas!" We often abbreviate our own or each other's names, unless mothers don't let us, so Beatrice becomes Bea, Tamara becomes Tammy, Susan becomes Sue, John becomes Jack, and Thomas becomes Tom. We call these pet names or nicknames, but what about the name of God? Should we call Christ "X"? What kind of respect should be given to God's name? The Hebrew people felt such respect and fear for the name of God that they would not speak or write it. Thomas Cahill explains, "Only the high priest could pronounce the name of God—and only once a year in the prayer on the Day of Atonement. Many read 'Adonai' (the Lord) when they come to the word 'YHWH'" (*The Gifts of the Jews*).

"When Moses asked God about God's name, God said to Moses, "I am who I am" (Yahweh or YHWH), not giving Moses his name because God knew we would find some way to desecrate his name (Exodus 3:13–14). Tell this story of respect the next time you see Xmas and thank God we feel confident to utter his name, the Lord, God. Amen.

X-ray

We all have some idea what an X-ray is: an imaging tool that can penetrate solids, see into our bodies, and reveal smudges in tissue or breaks in bones. Imaging technology has recently made advances with a machine that peeks inside the heart. If that seems a good idea for medical treatment, well and good. However, on the spiritual level we may not be comfortable with people knowing what's really in our hearts, that is, our desires, loves, fears, motives, and so on. That's secret, sacred territory. Sometimes we even try to hide from God. How foolish! How futile to try to hide from God, who knows us inside and out. We cannot hide our deepest secrets, motives, sins, or fears from God. He sees everything. Remember how Jesus looked into the heart of the Samaritan woman (John 4:1–26)? "Open up" to the eyes of God and to the healing "rays" of God's brilliance. Let his touch heal any broken or smudged places.

My Journal

- Sit in silence and ask the Spirit to come into your mind and heart, fill you with his fire, inspire you with wisdom and light, and show you visions you dream of!

- Where do you need God's healing touch in your life? How can you offer the healing of forgiveness or care to someone in your life?

Mary said, "Here I am,
the servant of the Lord,
let it be with me
according to your word."

LUKE 1:38

Yes

"Yes" is a nod of the head, a thumbs-up, a wink of an eye, a smile or grin, a positive word, or a loving tone of voice. We express a willingness to believe something we cannot see. We support someone's world and allow dreams to begin to breathe, helping bring them to fulfillment. With our yes, we can give love to someone who needs us desperately. We can raise shoulders and spirits. With our yes we let balloons fly. We can give voice to others and help them. We can give them life. We can save piles of books, old buildings, and bundles of kittens with a nod of our head or a simple yes. We have so much power!

Used properly, "yes" is one of the most valuable words in the English language. A loving yes can build the confidence of teenagers and strengthen the self-esteem that enables them to say no to drugs, cheating, lying, or other hurtful or self-destructive behavior that teenagers are drawn to. Saying yes with positive reinforcement can lead to a teenager saying yes to growth. Despite their fear, Noah,

Joseph, Moses, David, Mary, and Jesus' disciples said yes. Their assent changed their lives and our lives. Thank God for giving us free will to choose between no and yes. Now use the word "yes" and exercise your power.

Yesterday

Learn from yesterday. Then forget yesterday. God has.

My Journal

- How can you use "yes" to affirm others?

- What might God be asking you to say "yes" to in your life?

Jesus said, "Today salvation has come to this house."

LUKE 19:9

Zacchaeus

So many times we think we are too short, too fat, or too weak to do anything to achieve honor or high praise. One day as Jesus was entering a town, a short tax collector named Zacchaeus stood in a crowd, but he could not see over the heads of those in front of him, so he climbed a tree to see Jesus. Can you imagine his surprise, thinking he was the one climbing up to see Jesus, when Jesus stopped and looked up. He called out to Zacchaeus with some urgency, "Zacchaeus, come down immediately. I must stay at your house today." Zacchaeus, being so sought out, quaking because the Lord said he must stay at his house, immediately repented of his past sins and offered to repay four times over the amount for any cheating he had done. Jesus honored Zacchaeus by stating, "This man too is a son of Abraham." A short, wealthy tax collector is saved just as a poor and humble child of Israel is, if he seeks God and repents.

Zacchaeus' story offers sharp contrast to the rich man who asked Jesus for salvation, but was unwilling to humble himself and give up his wealth and many treasures. Jesus said of him, "How hard it is for those who have wealth to enter the kingdom of God!" (Luke 19:1–10; 18:24).

Don't wait for Jesus to walk by you. Climb a tree to seek him out. Then give up those impediments that burden you. Seek forgiveness from those you have cheated, and humbly trust in the Lord. You are a chosen child of God who promised you the kingdom.

My Journal

- Reflect on the gospel passage about Zacchaeus. How does its message apply to you?

We are at the close of *Alphabet Soup for Christian Living*. You have read about some people and things of God. Perhaps you have been inspired with a few new ideas, or you were stimulated to some discussion, or you remembered things you had not thought of in a long time. Let us stop here together for a moment before closing this book and thank God for the gifts that the Holy Spirit gives to us. For some, the gift of the Spirit is the gift of creation with pen and ink; for others, it is the gift of a great voice, or the ability to build with brick and stone. For some, it means being a teacher who encourages young minds to love knowledge. Use of our gifts requires a healthy amount of courage and love. Ask daily for the courage to use the gifts that the Holy Spirit lovingly pours out on us.

Resources

Benedict J. Groeschel. *The Journey toward God.* Ann Arbor: Servant Publications, 2000.

Margaret Guenther. *Holy Listening: The Art of Spiritual Direction.* Cambridge, MA: Cowley Publications, 1992.

Thomas Cahill. *The Gifts of the Jews: How a Tribe of Desert Nomads Changed the Way Everyone Thinks.* New York: Anchor Books, 1998.

Mitch Finley. *The Joy of Being a Eucharistic Minister.* Totowa, NJ: Resurrection Press, 1998.

Joseph Bernardin. *The Gift of Peace.* Chicago: Loyola University Press, 1997.

Henri Nouwen. *Heart Speaks to Heart.* Notre Dame, IN: Ave Maria Press, 1989.

Bruce Wilkinson. *Secrets of the Vine.* Sisters, OR: Multnomah, 2001.